60 Quick Knit BABY Essentials

SWEATERS, TOYS, BLANKETS, & MORE IN CHERUB™ FROM CASCADE YARNS®

THE EDITORS OF SIXTH&SPRING BOOKS

 sixth&springbooks NEW YORK

sixth&springbooks

161 Avenue of the Americas, New York, NY 10013
sixthandspringbooks.com

Managing Editor	Page Layout	Vice President
LAURA COOKE	EMILY JONES	TRISHA MALCOLM
Senior Editor	Supervising	Publisher
LISA SILVERMAN	Patterns Editor	CAROLINE KILMER
	LORI STEINBERG	
Art Director		Production Manager
DIANE LAMPHRON	Patterns Editors	DAVID JOINNIDES
	LISA BUCCELLATO	
Yarn Editor	PAT HARSTE	President
VANESSA PUTT	MARI LYNN PATRICK	ART JOINNIDES
	MARGEAU SOBOTI	
Editorial Assistant		Chairman
JOHANNA LEVY	Photography	JAY STEIN
	JACK DEUTSCH	
	Stylist	
	JOANNA RADOW	

Library of Congress Cataloging-in-Publication Data
60 quick knit baby essentials : sweaters, toys, blankets, and more in Cherub from Cascade Yarns / the editors of Sixth&Spring Books. — First edition.
pages cm
ISBN 978-1-936096-83-1
1. Knitting—Patterns. 2. Infants' supplies. 3. Infants' clothing. I. Sixth & Spring Books. II. Cascade Yarns. III. Title: Sixty quick knit baby essentials.
TT825.A12487 2015   746.43'2—dc23   2014030161

MANUFACTURED IN CHINA
1 3 5 7 9 10 8 6 4 2
First Edition

CASCADE YARNS
DISTRIBUTOR OF FINE YARN

cascadeyarns.com

contents

Check It Out!

Turn to the inside back
cover to find abbreviations,
an explanation of
skill levels, and even
a handy ruler!

INTRODUCTION

Mini Must-Haves

In this book the bestselling 60 Quick Knits series returns to the world of baby knits, with a brand-new yarn and a whole new batch of adorable designs.

Following on the success of *60 Quick Baby Knits*, *60 More Quick Baby Knits*, and *60 Quick Baby Blankets*, we bring you our most impressive collection yet of patterns for little ones. From animal blankets to Aran sweaters; from adorable toys to cozy hats and booties, you'll find designs for every level of ability and every style, from some of today's most talented designers.

Every project in these pages has been designed especially for Cascade's new Cherub line of yarns, a super-soft, easy-care blend that comes in multiple weights and in solid and variegated colors—perfect for creating cherished, long-lasting baby knits.

 To locate retailers that carry Cascade Cherub, visit cascadeyarns.com.

Sparkle Snowflake Booties

These tall booties with Fair Isle snowflakes and pompom ties will stay on baby's feet and keep them toasty on the coldest of days.

DESIGNED BY LISA SILVERMAN

Sizes
Instructions are written for size 3–6 months.

Knitted Measurements
Length, cuff to heel (cuff folded)
5"/12.5cm
Length, heel to toe 4"/10cm

Materials
- 1 3½oz/100g skein (each approx 240yd/220m) of Cascade Yarns *Cherub Aran Sparkle* (nylon/acrylic/metallic) each in #203 silver (MC) and #201 white (CC)
- One set (5) each sizes 5 and 6 (3.75 and 4mm) double-pointed needles (dpns) *or size to obtain gauge*
- Stitch markers

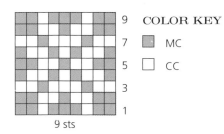

9 sts

COLOR KEY
- 9
- 7 ▨ MC
- 5 ☐ CC
- 3
- 1

Note
Sole is worked in rows; sts are picked up to work foot and leg in the rnd.

Bootie
SOLE
With larger needles and MC, cast on 8 sts.
Next row (WS) Purl.
Next (inc) row (RS) K1, M1, k to last st, M1, k1—10 sts.
Next (inc) row (WS) P1, M1, p to last st, M1, p1—12 sts.
Cont in St st until piece measures 3"/7.5cm, end with a WS row.
Next (dec) row K1, ssk, k to last 3 sts, k2tog, k1—2 sts dec'd.
Rep dec row every other row once more—8 sts. Leave on needle.

BEGIN FOOT
With RS facing, larger needles, and MC, pick up and k 44 sts evenly along entire edge of sole to beg of sole, k 4 sole sts, place marker (pm) for beg of rnd—52 sts. Divide sts on dpns. P 1 rnd. K 3 rnds.

SHAPE FOOT
Set-up rnd K23, pm, k6, pm, p to end.
Next (dec) rnd K to 2 sts before marker, k2tog, sl marker, k6, sl marker, ssk, k to end—2 sts dec'd.
Rep dec rnd every rnd twice more—6 sts.

Next (dec) rnd K to 3 sts before next marker, k3tog, sl marker, k6, sl marker, sssk, k to end—4 sts dec'd.
Rep dec rnd every rnd 3 times more—30 sts. Knit 4 rnds, removing all markers except for beg-of-rnd marker.

BEGIN CHART
Set-up rnd K3, pm, k9, pm, k6, pm, k9, pm, k3.
Next rnd K3, sl marker, work rnd 1 of chart over 9 sts, sl marker, k6, sl marker, work rnd 1 over 9 sts, sl marker, k3.
Cont to work chart in this manner until rnd 9 of chart is complete. With MC, knit 3 rnds. Change to smaller needles.

CUFF
With CC, knit 1 rnd.
Next rnd *K1, p1; rep from * around.
Rep this rnd for k1, p1 rib until cuff measures 1½"/4cm. Bind off.

Finishing
I-CORD TIE
With smaller dpns and CC, cast on 3 sts. *K3, slide sts to opposite end of needle to work next row from RS, pulling yarn tightly across WS; rep from * until cord measures 14½"/37cm. With CC, make two 1"/2.5cm pompoms and fasten to end of each cord. Fold cuff. Wrap cord around ankle and tie in bow. ∎

22 sts and 31 rows/rnds to 4"/10cm over St st using size 6 (4mm) needles. *Take time to check gauge.*

Striped Hat & Mitten Set

Grab your favorite colors and whip up a quick, cute,
and useful gift for expecting parents.

DESIGNED BY MARGEAU SOBOTI

■◧▢▢

Knitted Measurements
HAT
Head circumference 13½"/34.5cm
Length 5½"/14cm

MITTENS
Hand circumference 4"/10cm
Length 4½"/11cm

Materials
■ 1 3½oz/100g skein (each approx
240yd/220m) of Cascade Yarns Cherub
Aran (nylon/acrylic) each in #34 classic
blue (A), #28 boy blue (B), and #8 baby
blue (C) OR #30 violet (A), #16 lavender
(B), and #07 baby lavender (C)

■ One pair size 6 (4mm) needles or *size
to obtain gauge*

Stripe Pattern
2 rows A, 2 rows B, 2 rows C.
Rep these 6 rows for stripe pat.

Hat
With A, cast on 78 sts.
Next row (RS) *K1, p1; rep from * to end
for k1, p1 rib.
Cont in k1, p1 rib until piece measures
1"/2.5cm from beg, end with a RS row.
Next row (WS) Purl, dec 1 st evenly
across—77 sts.

BEGIN STRIPE PAT
Work in St st (k on RS, p on WS) and stripe
pat until piece measures 4"/10cm from
beg, end with a WS row.

SHAPE CROWN
Next (dec) row (RS) [K5, k2tog]
11 times—66 sts.
Purl 1 row.
Next (dec) row (RS) [K4, k1 tog]
11 times—55 sts.
Purl 1 row.
Cont in this manner, working 1 less st
before the k2tog, every other row 3 times
more—22 sts.
Purl 1 row.
Next (dec) row (RS) [K2tog] 11
times—11 sts.

Purl 1 row. Break yarn, leaving a long
tail. Thread tail through rem sts and
pull tight to close. Sew back seam,
being careful to match stripes.

Mittens
With A, cast on 26 sts. Work in
k1, p1 rib as for hat, for 8 rows.

BEGIN STRIPE PAT
Work in St st and stripe pat until
piece measures 3½"/9cm from beg,
end with a WS row.

SHAPE TOP
Next (dec) row (RS) K1, [ssk, k8,
k2tog] twice, k1—22 sts.
Purl 1 row.
Next (dec) row (RS) K1, [ssk, k6,
k2tog] twice, k1—18 sts.
Purl 1 row.
Next (dec) row (RS) K1, [ssk, k4,
k2tog] twice, k1—14 sts.
Purl 1 row.
Next (dec) row (RS) K1, [ssk, k2,
k2tog] twice, k1—10 sts.
Purl 1 row. Break yarn, leaving a long
tail. Thread tail through rem sts and
pull tight to close. Sew side seam,
being careful to match stripes. ■

Gauge
23 sts and 29 rows to 4"/10cm over St st using size 6 (4mm) needles.
Take time to check gauge.

Eyelet Stripe Jacket

Garter stripes and eyelets strike a balance in an easy button-down that's a great layer for cool spring nights.

DESIGNED BY BONNIE FRANZ

Sizes
Instructions are written for size 3 months (6 months, 12 months). Shown in size 6 months.

Knitted Measurements
Chest (closed) 18½ (20, 22½)"/47 (51, 57)cm
Length 8½ (9½, 10½)"/21.5 (24, 26.5)cm
Upper arm 8 (9, 10)"/20.5 (23, 25.5)cm

Materials
■ 1 1¾oz/50g skein (each approx 229yd/210m) of Cascade Yarns *Cherub Baby* (nylon/acrylic) each in #07 baby lavender (A), #05 baby mint (B), and #3 baby lime (C)

■ Size 3 (3.25mm) circular needle, 24"/60cm long, *or size to obtain gauge*

■ One pair size 3 (3.25mm) needles

■ One set (5) size 3 (3.25mm) double-pointed needles (dpns)

■ Stitch holder, stitch marker

■ 5 (6, 6) ⅝"/16mm buttons

Eyelet Pattern 1
(for body)
(multiple of 2 sts plus 2)
Rows 1–4 Knit.
Row 5 (RS) K1, *yo, k2tog; rep from *, end k1.
Rows 6–8 Knit.
Rep rows 1–8 for eyelet pat 1 for body.

Eyelet Pattern 2
(for sleeves)
(multiple of 2 sts plus 2)
Rnds 1 and 3 Knit.
Rnds 2 and 4 Purl.
Rnd 5 K1, *yo, k2tog; rep from * around, end k1.
Rnd 6 Purl.
Rnd 7 Knit.
Rnd 8 Purl.
Rep rnds 1–8 for eyelet pat 2 for sleeves.

Stripe Pattern
Working in eyelet pat, *work 8 rows A, 8 rows B, 8 rows C; rep from * (24 rows) for stripe pat.

Notes
1) Body is worked back and forth in one piece to the underarms.
2) Sleeves are worked in the round.

Cardigan Body
With circular needle and A, cast on 112 (120, 136) sts. Do not join; work back and forth. Work in stripe pat and eyelet pat 1 until piece measures 4½ (5, 5½)"/11.5 (12.5, 14)cm from beg, end with a WS row.

DIVIDE FOR FRONTS AND BACK
Change to straight needles.
Next row (RS) Work across first 28 (30, 34) sts, place these sts on holder for right front, work across next 56 (60, 68) sts (back); leave rem 28 (30, 34) sts on needle for left front.

BACK
Work even until armhole measures 4 (4½, 5)"/10 (11.5, 12.5)cm, end with a WS row. Bind off purlwise.

LEFT FRONT
Change to straight needles.
Next row (RS) Work 28 (30, 34) sts from needle. Work even until armhole measures 2½ (3, 3½)"/6.5 (7.5, 9)cm, end with a RS row.

Gauge
24 sts and 48 rows to 4"/10cm over eyelet pat using 3 (3.25mm) needles.
Take time to check gauge.

Eyelet Stripe Jacket

SHAPE NECK

Next row (WS) Bind off first 6 (7, 8) sts for front neck. Dec 1 st at neck edge on next row, then every other row 4 times more. Work even on 17 (18, 21) sts until piece measures same length as back to shoulder, end with a WS row. Bind off purlwise.

RIGHT FRONT

Place 28 (30, 34) sts from holder onto straight needle ready for a WS row. Work as for left front, reversing neck shaping by binding off at beg of next RS row. Sew shoulder seams.

SLEEVES

With RS facing, dpns, and A, beg at underarm and pick up and k 48 (54, 60) sts evenly spaced around entire armhole edge. Divide sts evenly between 4 needles. Join and place marker (pm) for beg of rnds. Beg with rnd 2, work in stripe pat and eyelet pat 2, work even for 6 rnds more.

Dec rnd K2tog, knit to 2 sts before marker, ssk—2 sts dec'd.

Rep dec rnd every 6th rnd 8 times more. Work even on 30 (36, 42) sts until piece measures 5 (5½, 6)"/12.5 (14, 15)cm from beg. Bind off knitwise.

Finishing

Lightly block piece to measurements.

RIGHT FRONT BAND

With RS facing, straight needles, and A, pick up and k 42 (48, 54) sts evenly spaced across right front edge. Knit 3 rows. Bind off all sts loosely knitwise.

LEFT FRONT BAND

Work as for right front.

NECKBAND

With RS facing, straight needles, and A, pick up and k 27 (28, 29) sts evenly spaced along right front edge, 22 (24, 26) sts across back neck edge, 27 (28, 29) sts along left front neck edge—76 (80, 84) sts. Knit next row. Bind off knitwise. Sew buttons on left front band for a girl or right front band for a boy as foll: sew first button to correspond to topmost eyelet closest to neck edge. Working toward bottom edge, *skip one stripe, then sew next button to correspond to next eyelet; rep from * 3 (4, 4) times more. ■

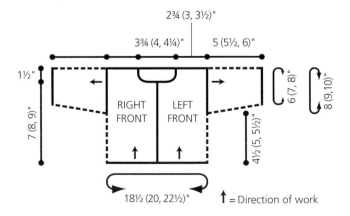

2¾ (3, 3½)"

3¾ (4, 4¼)"   5 (5½, 6)"

1½"

7 (8, 9)"

RIGHT FRONT   LEFT FRONT

6 (7, 8)"

8 (9,10)"

4½ (5, 5½)"

18½ (20, 22½)"   ↑ = Direction of work

Drifting Diamonds Dress

Worn on its own or layered for winter, this graphic Fair Isle dress is a modern baby's fashion statement!

DESIGNED BY LOIS S. YOUNG

Sizes

Instructions are written for size 6 months (12 months, 18 months). Shown in size 6 months.

Knitted Measurements

Chest 18½ (21¾, 22½)"/47 (54, 58)cm
Length 14 (16¾, 18)"/35.5 (42.5, 45.5)cm

Materials

■ 2 1¾oz/50g skeins (each approx 180yd/165m) of Cascade Yarns *Cherub DK* (nylon/acrylic) in #9 ecru (C)

■ 1 skein each in #34 classic blue (A) and #27 navy (B)

■ Two size 3 (3.25mm) circular needles, 24 and 16"/60 and 40cm long, *or size to obtain gauge*

■ One set (5) size 3 (3.25mm) double-pointed needles (dpns)

■ Stitch markers

Dress

With longer circular needle and A, cast on 168 (192, 204) sts. Join, being careful not to twist sts, and place marker (pm) for beg of rnd.
Knit 1 rnd, purl 1 rnd with A; knit 1 rnd, purl 1 rnd with B; knit 1 rnd, purl 1 rnd with A; knit 1 rnd, purl 1 rnd with C.

BEGIN CHART PATTERN

Note Chart is worked in St st (k every rnd).
Rnd 1 Work 6-st rep 28 (32, 54) times around.

Cont to work chart in this manner until rnd 8 is complete. Rep rnds 1–8 for 3 (5, 6) times more. Work rnds 9–20 twice, working 12-st rep 14 (16, 17) times around. Then, cont in this manner to work rnds 21–34 for 4 times. Knit 1 rnd with C. Piece measures approx 10 (12, 12½)"/25.5 (30.5, 31.5)cm from beg.
Next (dec) rnd *K2tog, k1; rep from * around—112 (128, 136) sts.
Purl 1 rnd with C. With A, knit 1 rnd, purl 1 rnd. With B, knit 1 rnd, purl 1 rnd 2 (4, 6) times.

DIVIDE FOR FRONT AND BACK

Note Cont to work the yoke in garter st in rows (k every row) with B only
Next row (RS) With B, bind off 5 (7, 7) sts, k until there are 46 (50, 54) sts on needle, bind off next 10 (14, 14) sts, k until there are 46 (50, 54) sts on needle, join a short length of B and bind off rem 5 (7, 7) sts. Working on 46 (50, 54) sts for back only, work as foll:
Next row (WS) Sl 1, k to end.
Next (dec) row (RS) [Sl 1, ssk] to last 3 sts, k2tog, k1—2 sts dec'd.
Rep last 2 rows 2 (3, 2) times more—40 (42, 48) sts. Work even until

Gauges

27 sts and 45 rows/rnds to 4"/10cm over chart pat using size 3 (3.25mm) needles.
24 sts and 48 rows/rnds to 4"/10cm over garter st using size 3 (3.25mm) needles. *Take time to check gauges.*

Drifting Diamonds Dress

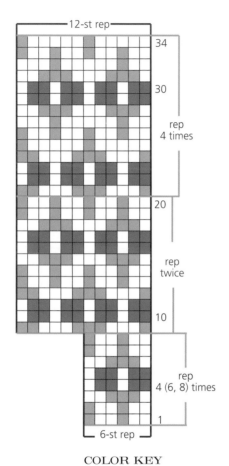

12-st rep

34
30
rep 4 times
20
rep twice
10
rep 4 (6, 8) times
1

6-st rep

COLOR KEY
A
B
C

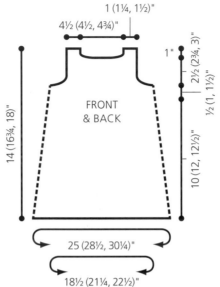

1 (1¼, 1½)"
4½ (4½, 4¾)"
1"
2½ (2¾, 3)"
½ (1, 1½)"
14 (16¾, 18)"
FRONT & BACK
10 (12, 12½)"
25 (28½, 30¼)"
18½ (21¼, 22½)"

armhole measures 2½ (2¾, 3)"/6.5 (7, 7.5)cm from the bind-off row. Pm to mark center 22 (22, 24) sts on last WS row.

SHAPE NECK
Next row (RS) Sl 1, k8 (9, 11), join a 2nd ball of yarn and bind off center 22 (22, 24) sts, k to end.
Working both sides at once with separate balls of yarn, cont to shape neck.
Next row (WS) Sl 1, k8 (9, 11); on 2nd side, k9 (10, 12).
Next (dec) row (RS) Sl 1, k to last 3 sts, k2tog, k1; on 2nd side, k1, ssk, k to end.
Next row Sl 1, k to end; on 2nd side, k to end.
Rep last 2 rows once more—7 (8, 10) sts each side.
Work even until armhole measures 3½ (3¾, 4)"/9 (9.5, 10)cm. Bind off sts on each side.
Rejoin yarn to 46 (50, 54) sts for front, ready to work a WS row, and complete as for back.

Finishing
Sew shoulder seams.
With dpns and A and RS facing, pick up and k 56 (60, 64) sts evenly around armhole edge. Bind off all sts purlwise on the RS. For the neck trim, with shorter circular needle and A, pick up and k 80 (80, 84) sts evenly around neck edge. Bind off all sts purlwise on the RS. ■

Mini Mouse Mittens

A sweet embroidered face and pink ears transform simple mittens into an adorable accessory.

DESIGNED BY AMY BAHRT

Size
Instructions are written for size 6–12 months.

Knitted Measurements
Hand circumference 4½"/11cm
Length 5"/12.5cm

Materials
■ 1 3½oz/100g skein (each approx 240yd/220m) of Cascade Yarns *Cherub Aran* (nylon/acrylic) each in #32 cotton candy (A) and #17 grey (B)

■ Small amount of #40 black (C)

■ One pair each sizes 5 and 7 (3.75 and 4.5mm) needles *or size to obtain gauge*

■ Scrap yarn

■ Embroidery needle

■ Stitch markers

Right Mitten
With smaller needles and A, cast on 24 sts.
Next row (RS) *K1, p1; rep from * to end.
Rep last row for k1, p1 rib. Break A.
With B, work k1, p1 rib for 6 rows more.
Change to larger needles.
With B, work 2 rows St st (k on RS, p on WS).

THUMB GUSSET
Next (inc) row (RS) K14, place marker (pm), M1, k1, M1, pm, k to end—26 sts.
Purl 1 row.
Next (inc) row K to marker, sl marker, M1, k to marker, M1, sl marker, k to end—2 sts inc'd.
Rep inc row every other row once more—30 sts. Purl 1 row.
Next row (RS) K to marker, remove marker, place 7 thumb sts on scrap yarn for thumb, cast on 1 st, k to end—24 sts.
Cont in St st until piece measures 4¼"/11cm from beg, end with a WS row.

SHAPE TOP
Next (dec) row (RS) *K2, k2tog; rep from * to end—18 sts.
Purl 1 row.
Next (dec) row *K1, k2tog; rep from * to end—12 sts.
Purl 1 row.
Next (dec) row [K2tog] 6 times across—6 sts. Break yarn, leaving a long tail. Thread tail through rem sts and pull tightly to close.

THUMB
Place thumb sts on needle, ready to work a RS row.
Next row (RS) K6, M1, k1—8 sts.
Work even in St st until thumb measures 1"/2.5cm, end with a WS row.
Next row [K2tog] 4 times. Break yarn, leaving a long tail. Thread tail through rem 4 sts and pull tightly to close.
Sew thumb seam. Sew hand seam.

Finishing
EAR
With smaller needles and A, cast on 6 sts. Knit 1 row.
Work in garter st (k every row), inc 1 st each side every other row twice—10 sts. Work 4 rows even. Dec 1 st each side every other row twice—6 sts. Bind off.
With embroidery needle and A, work chain st embroidery around entire ear. Using photo as guide, sew ear to back of hand approx 1½"/4cm above thumb opening and 2"/5cm back from top of fingers. With black yarn, using photo as guide, embroider nose and whiskers using straight sts and eye using French knot.

Left Mitten
Work as for right mitten to thumb gusset.
Next (inc) row (RS) K9, pm, M1, k1, M1, pm, k to end.
Complete as for right mitten. ■

Gauge
18 sts and 26 rows to 4"/10cm over St st using larger needles.
Take time to check gauge.

Sweet Swing Cardigan

A simple cardi gets a beauty boost from a satin ribbon bow and a swingy A-line shape.

DESIGNED BY KATHERINE MEHLS

Sizes

Instructions are written for size 3 months (6 months, 12 months). Shown in size 6 months.

Knitted Measurements

Chest (closed) 25½ (28½, 31½)"/64.5 (72, 80)cm
Length 9 (10, 11)"/23 (25.5, 28)cm
Upper arm 6¼ (7, 8)"/16 (18, 20.5)cm

Materials

- 2 (2, 3) 1¾oz/50g skeins (each approx 229yd/210m) of Cascade Yarns *Cherub Baby* (nylon/acrylic) in #04 baby pink
- Size 4 (3.5mm) circular needle, 24"/61cm long, *or size to obtain gauge*
- One set (5) size 4 (3.5mm) double-pointed needles (dpns)
- Stitch holders, stitch markers
- 1yd/1m of ⅝"/16mm wide satin ribbon
- Sewing needle and thread to match

Stitch Glossary

M1R (make 1 right) Insert LH needle from back to front under the horizontal strand between the last st worked and the next st on LH needle. Knit this strand through the front loop to twist the st.
M1L (make 1 left) Insert LH needle from front to back under the horizontal strand between the last st worked and the next st on LH needle. Knit this strand through the back loop to twist the st.
kfb Inc 1 by knitting into the front and back of the next st.

Notes

1) Yoke and body are worked back and forth in one piece from the neck down.
2) Sleeves are worked in the round.

Cardigan Yoke

Beg at neck edge, work as foll:

NECKBAND/RIBBON CASING
With circular needle, cast on 62 (70, 78) sts. Do not join. Work back and forth as foll:
Row 1 (RS) K4, place marker (pm), k to last 4 sts, pm, k4.
Row 2 K4, sl marker, purl to last marker, sl marker, k4. Keeping 4 sts each side in garter st (knit every row) and rem sts in St st (k on RS, p on WS), work even for 10 rows more, end with a WS row.
Next (eyelet) row (RS) K7 (9, 8), [k2tog, yo, k7 (8, 10)] 5 times, k2tog, yo, k8 (9, 8).
Next row K4, sl marker, purl to last marker, sl marker, k4. Work even for 2 rows more.

BEG YOKE AND RAGLAN ARMHOLE SHAPING
Row 1 (inc RS) K4, sl marker, k9 (10, 11), M1R, pm, k2, pm, M1L, k6 (8, 10), M1R, pm, k2, pm, M1L, k16 (18, 20), M1R, pm, k2, pm, M1L, k6 (8, 10), M1R, pm, k2, pm, M1L, k9 (10, 11), sl marker, k4—70 (78, 86) sts.
Row 2 (WS) K4, purl to last 4 sts, k4.
Row 3 (inc) K4, [kfb] 9 (10, 11) times, k1, M1R, sl marker, k2, sl marker, M1L, k8 (10, 12), M1R, sl marker, k2, sl marker, M1L, k1, [kfb] 16 (18, 20) times, k1, M1R, sl marker, k2, sl marker, M1L, k8 (10, 12), M1R, sl marker, k2, sl marker, M1L, k1, [kfb] 9 (10, 11) times, sl marker, k4—112 (124, 136) sts.
Row 4 K4, purl to last 4 sts, k4.

Gauge

27 sts and 32 rows to 4"/10cm over St st using size 4 (3.5mm) needles. *Take time to check gauge.*

Sweet Swing Cardigan

sl marker, k2, sl marker, M1L, k1 [k1, kfb] 9 (10, 11) times, k1, sl marker, k4—156 (172, 188) sts.

Row 6 K4, purl to last 4 sts, k4.

Row 7 (inc) K4, sl marker, [k to next marker, M1R, sl marker, k2, sl marker, M1L] 4 times, k to last marker, sl marker, k4.

Row 8 K4, purl to last 4 sts, k4.
Rep last 2 rows 11 (13, 15) times more—252 (284, 316) sts.

DIVIDE FOR BODY AND SLEEVES

Next row (RS) K 47 (52, 57) sts (left front), place next 38 (44, 50) sts on holder (left sleeve), cast on 4 sts (left underarm), k 82 (92, 102) sts (back), place next 38 (44, 50) sts on holder (right sleeve), cast on 4 sts (right underarm), k 47 (52, 57) sts (right front)—184 (204, 224) sts.

BODY

Next row (WS) K4, purl to last 4 sts, k4. Cont to keep 4 sts each side in garter st and rem sts in St st, work even until piece measures 4¾ (5¼, 5¾)"/12 (13.5, 14.5)cm from underarm

cast-on, end with a RS row. Cont in garter st on all sts for ¾"/2cm, end with a RS row. Bind off loosely knitwise.

SLEEVES

With RS facing and dpns, skip first 2 sts of underarm cast-on, pick up and k 1 st in each of next 2 sts, k 38 (44, 50) sts from sleeve holder, pick up and k 1 st in each rem 2 sts of underarm cast-on—42 (48, 54) sts.

Divide sts evenly on 4 needles. Join and pm for beg of rnds. Work around in St st (knit every rnd) for 3 (3½, 4)"/7.5 (9, 10)cm. Cont in garter st (k one rnd, p one rnd) for ½"/1.5cm.
Bind off knitwise.

Finishing

Lightly block piece to measurements. For ribbon casing, fold neckband in half to WS and whipstitch in place. Insert ribbon into casing and weave through eyelets. Tie ribbon in a bow, then trim ribbon ends (if desired). Using sewing thread and needle, tack ribbon in place at each front garter stitch band, working through all thicknesses. ■

Row 5 (inc) K4, sl marker, k1, [k1, kfb] 9 (10, 11) times, k1, M1R, sl marker, k2, sl marker, M1L, k10 (12, 14), M1R, sl marker, k2, sl marker, M1L, k1, [k1, kfb] 18 (20, 22) times, k1, M1R, sl marker, k2, sl marker, M1L, k10 (12, 14), M1R,

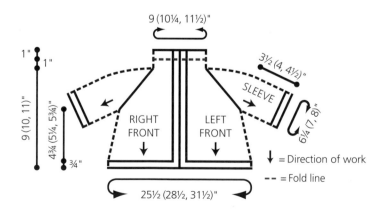

Pinstripe Blocks Blanket

Garter stitch stripes run every which way in squares
that are picked up and knit as you go.

DESIGNED BY KATHARINE HUNT

Knitted Measurements
Approx 32 x 38"/81 x 96.5cm

Materials
■ 4 3½oz/100g skeins (each approx
240yd/220m) of Cascade Yarns *Cherub
Aran* (nylon/acrylic) in #09 ecru (A)

■ 2 skeins each in #12 turquoise (B)
and #13 jade (C)

■ One pair size 6 (4mm) needles *or size
to obtain gauge*

■ Size 6 (4mm) circular needle,
32"/80cm long

■ Scrap yarn for holding sts

Notes
1) Blanket is worked in squares which
are picked up and knit from the square
previously worked and joined together
as you work.
2) The central block of 16 squares is
worked without breaking A.
3) Blanket is worked in garter st
(k every row).
4) See diagram for square placement.

Blanket
SQUARE 1
With A, cast on 33 sts. Knit 1 (WS) row
for 1st stripe.
Join B and work 2 rows B, 2 rows A until
32 stripes have been worked. With A,
knit 1 row.
Place sts on scrap yarn to hold.

SQUARE 2
With A and RS facing, pick up and k 33
sts along edge of square just worked.
Knit 1 (WS) row for 1st stripe.
Join C and work 2 rows C, 2 rows A until
32 stripes have been worked. With A,
knit 1 row.
Place sts on scrap yarn to hold.

SQUARE 3
With A and B, work as for square 2.

SQUARE 4 (JOIN CAST-ON EDGE)
With A and RS facing, pick up and k 33
sts along edge of square just worked,
pick up and k 1 st along cast-on edge of
square 1, with free needle, pass the 2nd
st on the LH needle over the stitch picked
up in the cast-on row. With A, knit 1
(WS) row for 1st stripe.

Gauge
20 sts and 40 rows to 4"/10cm over garter st using size 6 (4mm) needles.
Take time to check gauge.

Pinstripe Blocks Blanket

Next (joining) row (RS) With C, k to last st, sl 1, pick up and k 1 st from cast-on edge, sl 2 sl sts back to LH needle and ssk (slipped st with picked-up st).
Next row Knit.
Cont to work in this way, working 2-row stripes of A and C, and joining to cast-on edge every RS row, until 32 stripes have been worked. With A, work 1 more joining row. Place sts on scrap yarn to hold.

SQUARE 5
With A and RS facing, pick up and k 33 sts along edge of square 1. Complete as for square 1 with A and C.

SQUARE 6
With A and B, work as for square 2.

SQUARE 7 (JOIN LEFT SIDE)
With A and RS facing, pick up and k 33 sts along edge of square just worked, place next st from scrap yarn holding square 1 sts on needle and pass last picked-up st over it. With A, knit 1 (WS) row for 1st stripe.
Next (joining) row (RS) With C, k to last st, ssk (last st with next held st).
Next row Knit.
Cont to work in this way, working 2-row stripes of A and C and joining to held sts every RS row, until 32 stripes have been worked. With A, work 1 more joining row. Place sts on scrap yarn to hold.

SQUARE 8 (JOIN RIGHT SIDE)
With RS facing, place last st of previous square worked on RH needle, with A, pick up and k 1 st along edge of adjacent square, pass held st over picked-up st, pick up and k 32 more sts along edge of adjacent square.
With A, knit 1 (WS) row for 1st stripe.
Next (joining) row (RS) With B, k next held st tog with first st, k to end of row.
Cont to work in this way, working 2-row stripes of A and B, and joining to cast-on edge every RS row, until 32 stripes have been worked. With A, work 1 more joining row. Place sts on scrap yarn to hold.

SQUARE 9
Work as for square 2.

SQUARE 10
With A and B, work as for square 7, using held square 2 sts.

SQUARE 11
With A and C, work as for square 8.

SQUARE 12
With A and B, work as for square 2.

SQUARE 13
With A and C, work as for square 7.

SQUARE 14
With A and B, work as for square 8.

SQUARE 15
With A and C, work as for square 2.

SQUARE 16
With A and B, work as for square 7. When square is complete, break A, leaving a long tail. With tail, sew open sts to corresponding edge of square 5.

SQUARE 17
With A, cast on 33 sts. With A and C, complete as for square 7, joining to edge of square 12.

SQUARE 18
With A, pick up and k 22 sts along edge of square 13. With A and B, complete as for square 8.

SQUARE 19
With A and C, work as for square 7.

SQUARE 20
With A, pick up and k 33 sts along edge of square 15. With A and B, complete as for square 8.
Do not break A.

Finishing
BORDER
With RS facing, circular needle and A, pick up and k 165 sts evenly along 1 long edge.
Next (inc) row (WS) K1, kfb, k to last 2 sts, kfb, k1—2 sts inc'd.
Next row Knit.
Cont in garter st, rep inc row every other row twice more.
Cont to rep inc row every WS row, work in stripe pat as foll: 6 rows B, 6 rows A, 6 rows C, 6 rows A. Bind off.
Rep for opposite long edge.
With RS facing, circular needle and A, pick up and k 132 sts evenly along 1 short edge. Work as for long edge.
Rep for opposite short edge.
Sew corners of border tog. ∎

Just-Right Ribbed Booties

Ribbed cuffs and soles and a crochet chain tie help keep these booties snug and warm on baby's feet.

DESIGNED BY ROSEMARY DRYSDALE

Size
Instructions are written for size 3–6 months.

Knitted Measurements
Ankle circumference 5"/12.5cm
Length from heel to toe 3¾"/9.5cm

Materials
- 1 1¾oz/50g skein (each approx 180yd/165m) of Cascade Yarns *Cherub DK* (nylon/acrylic) in #20 denim
- One pair size 4 (3.5mm) needles *or size to obtain gauge*
- Size E/4 (3.5mm) crochet hook (for tie)

Booties
Cast on 31 sts. Purl 1 (WS) row.
Row 1 (RS) [K1, kfb, *p1, k1; rep from * 6 times more, kfb] twice, k1—35 sts.
Row 2 and all WS rows Purl.
Row 3 [K1, kfb, *k1, p1; rep from * 7 times more, kfb] twice, k1—39 sts.
Row 5 [K1, kfb, *p1, k1; rep from * 8 times more, kfb] twice, k1—43 sts.
Row 7 [K1, kfb, *k1, p1; rep from * 9 times more, kfb] twice, k1—47 sts.
Row 9 [P1, k1] 12 times, k1, [P1, k1] 11 times.
Next (dec) row (RS) K2tog tbl, [p1, k1] 10 times, [k1, p1] 11 times, k1, k2tog—45 sts.
Purl 1 row.

INSTEP
Row 1 (RS) K27, k2tog tbl, turn.
Row 2 Sl 1, p9, p2tog, turn.
Row 3 Sl 1, k9, k2tog tbl, turn.
Rep rows 2 and 3 for 5 times more, then rep row 2 once more—31 sts, 10 sts on each side of 11 instep sts.
Next row (RS) Sl 1, k20.
Next row P to end.
Work 2 rows in St st (k on RS, p on WS).

LEG
Eyelet row (RS) *K1, yo, k2tog; rep from * to last st, k1.
Work 3 rows in St st.
Next row (RS) *K1, p1; rep from * to last st, k1.
K the knit sts and p the purl sts for k1, p1 rib for 11 rows more.
Next (turning) row (RS) Knit.

CUFF
Note that RS of cuff is WS of bootie.
Next row (RS) *K1, p1; rep from * to last st, k1.
Next row Purl.
Rep last 2 rows 10 times more.
Bind off in rib.

Finishing
Fold in half and sew seam from turning row to toe. Fold cuff to RS at turning row.

TIES (MAKE 2)
With crochet hook, ch 64. Fasten off. Thread chain through eyelets and tie in bow. ■

Gauge
24 sts and 32 rows/rnds to 4"/10cm over St st using size 4 (3.5mm) needles.
Take time to check gauge.

Bunny Romper

With its ruffled skirt and textured intarsia bunny, this romper
is ready to steal the summer spotlight.

DESIGNED BY SANDI PROSSER

■■■■

Sizes
Instructions are written for size 3 months
(6 months, 12 months). Shown in size 6
months.

Knitted Measurements
Chest 19 (21, 23)"/48 (53.5, 58.5)cm
Hips 22 (24, 26)"/56 (61, 66)cm
Length 14 (15, 16)"/35.5 (38, 40.5)cm

Materials
■ 2 (2, 3) 1¾oz/50g skeins (each approx
180yd/165m) of Cascade Yarns *Cherub
DK* (nylon/acrylic) in #05 baby mint (A)

■ 1 skein each in #32 cotton candy (B)
and #14 melon (C)

■ One pair each sizes 3 and 4 (3.25 and
3.5mm) needles *or size to obtain gauge*

■ Size 4 (3.5mm) circular needle,
24"/60cm long

■ One extra size 4 needle

■ Stitch markers

■ Bobbins (optional)

■ Four ½"/12mm buttons

Seed Stitch
(over an odd number of sts)
Row 1 (RS) *K1, p1; rep from * to last st,
k1.
Row 2 K the purl and p the knit sts.
Rep row 2 for seed st.

Note
Bunny is worked using intarsia method.
Use a separate bobbin or strand for each
color section. Do not carry colors across
WS of work.

Romper Back
With circular needle and C, cast on 106
(116, 124) sts for ruffle. Do not join.
Next row (RS) *K1, p1; rep from *, end
p1 (k1, p1).
Next row (WS) Purl.
Cont in St st until ruffle measures 2¼
(2½, 2½)"/5 (6.5, 6.5)cm from beg, end
with a WS row, and 0 (1, 0) st in last
row—106 (115, 124) sts.
Next (dec) row (RS) K1, *k2tog, k1; rep
from * to end—71 (77, 83) sts. Break
yarn. Leave sts on needle.

Left Leg
With smaller needles and A, cast on 34
(36, 40) sts. Work 4 rows in seed stitch,
inc 2 (3, 2) sts evenly spaced on last

(WS) row—36 (39, 42) sts. Change to
larger needles.
Work 2 rows in St st.

SHAPE LEG
Inc 1 st at beg of next row, then every
4th row 3 times more—40 (43, 46) sts.
Work even in St st until piece measures
3¾ (4, 4½)"/9.5 (10, 11.5)cm from beg,
end with a WS row. Set piece aside.

Right Leg
Work as for left leg, reversing shaping
by working incs at ends of rows. Leave
sts on needle.

JOIN LEGS
Next (joining) row (RS) K 39 (42, 45)
sts from right leg, place marker (pm),
knit tog last st of right leg with first st
of left leg, k 39 (42, 45) sts from left
leg—79 (85, 91) sts.
Next row (WS) Purl.
Next (dec) row (RS) Knit to 2 sts
before marker, SKP, sl marker, k1,
k2tog, knit to end of row—77 (83,
89) sts.
Knit 1 row.
Rep last 2 rows 3 times more—71
(77, 83) sts. Remove marker.

Gauge
26 sts and 34 rows to 4"/10cm over St st using size 4 (3.5mm) needles. *Take time to check gauge.*

Bunny Romper

JOIN RUFFLE

Hold the ruffle and leg tog with needles parallel and ruffle in front, both ready for a RS row. With smaller needle and A, *insert RH needle knitwise into first st of both the front and back needle and knit them tog; rep from * until all sts are joined—71 (77, 83) sts. Change to larger needles.

BODY

Next row (WS) Purl.
Work 4 rows in St st.

SHAPE SIDES

Next (dec) row (RS) K2, k2tog, knit to last 4 sts, SKP, k2—69 (75, 81) sts.
Rep dec row every 8th row 3 times more—63 (69, 75) sts.
Work even in St st until piece measures 4 (4½, 5)"/10 (11.5, 12.5)cm from ruffle joining row, end with a WS row.

DIVIDE FOR BACK NECK

Next row (RS) K 30 (33, 36) sts, join 2nd ball of A, bind off 3 sts, work to end—30 (33, 36) sts each side.
Working both sides at once with separate balls of yarn, cont in St st until piece measures 6 (6½, 7)"/15.5 (16.5, 18)cm from ruffle joining row, end with a WS row.

SHAPE ARMHOLES

Next row (RS) Bind off 3 (4, 4) sts for armhole, work to end over both sides.
Next row (WS) Bind off 3 (4, 4) sts for armhole, work to end over both sides—27 (29, 32) sts each side.

Dec 1 st at armhole edges every row 3 times, then every other row 3 times—21 (23, 26) sts each side.
Work even until armholes measure 4¼ (4½, 4¾)"/10 (11, 12)cm, end with a WS row. Bind off.

Front

Work as for back to shape sides—71 (77, 83) sts.

BEGIN CHART

Next (dec) row (RS) K2, k2tog, k14 (17, 20), pm, work row 1 of chart from right to left over next 34 sts, pm, k15 (18, 21), SKP, k2—69 (75, 81) sts.
Next row (WS) P to marker, work row 2 of chart from left to right to next marker, p to end.
Cont to work chart in this manner through row 52, AT THE SAME TIME, cont side shaping and work armhole shaping as for back—45 (49, 55) sts.
Work even in A until armhole measures 2"/5cm, end with a WS row.

SHAPE NECK

Next row (RS) K17, join 2nd ball of A, bind off next 11 (15, 21) sts, work to end—17 sts each side.
Working both sides at once, dec 1 st at neck edge every row 3 times, then every other row 3 times more—11 sts each side.
Work even until armhole measures same as back to shoulder. Bind off.

Finishing

Lightly block to measurements.
Sew shoulder seams.

NECKBAND

With smaller needles, RS facing, and A, pick up and k 71 (79, 87) sts evenly along neckline. Work 4 rows in seed st, end with a RS row. Bind off.

BUTTON BAND

With smaller needles, RS facing, and A, pick up and k 51 (53, 55) sts along right side of back opening. Work 4 rows in seed st. Bind off.

BUTTONHOLE BAND

With smaller needles, RS facing, and A, pick up and k 51 (53, 55) sts along left side of back neck opening. Work 2 rows in seed st.
Next (buttonhole) row (WS) Work 4 sts, [yo, p2tog, work 10 (10, 11) sts] 3 times, yo, p2tog, work to end of row.
Work 1 row in seed st. Bind off.

ARMBANDS

With smaller needles, RS facing, and A, pick up and k 67 (71, 75) sts evenly along armhole opening. Work 4 rows in seed st. Bind off.

Finishing

Sew side and leg seams, including armbands and avoiding ruffle. Sew ruffle side seams. Sew crotch seam.
Sew buttons opposite buttonholes.
Using photo as guide and A, embroider 3 French knots for eyes and nose; then 2 straight st whiskers on either side of nose. ■

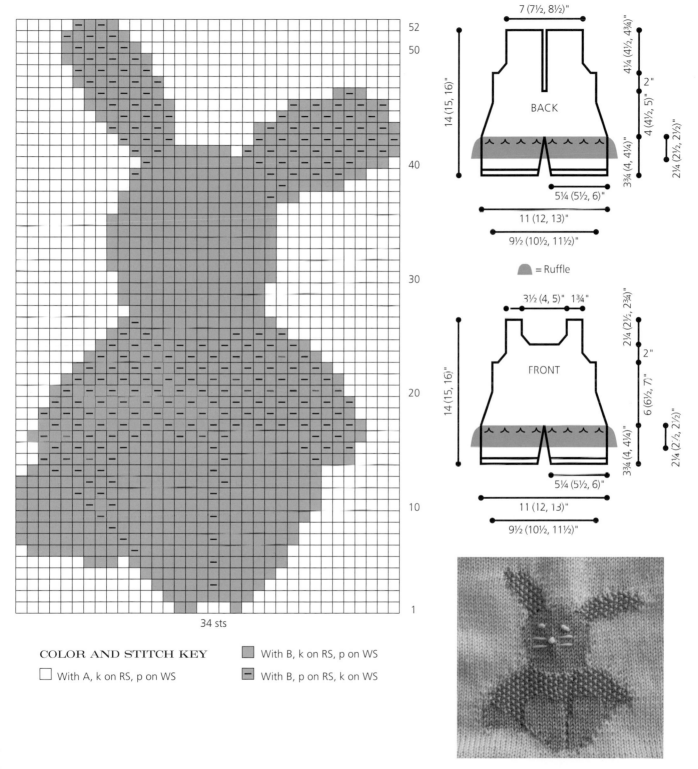

52
50

40

30

20

10

1

34 sts

7 (7½, 8½)"

14 (15, 16)"

4¼ (4½, 4¾)"
2"
4 (4½, 5)"

2¼ (2½, 2½)"

BACK

3¾ (4, 4¼)"

5¼ (5½, 6)"

11 (12, 13)"

9½ (10½, 11½)"

= Ruffle

3½ (4, 5)"   1¾"

14 (15, 16)"

2¼ (2½, 2¾)"
2"
6 (6½, 7)"

2¼ (2½, 2½)"

FRONT

3¾ (4, 4¼)"

5¼ (5½, 6)"

11 (12, 13)"

9½ (10½, 11½)"

COLOR AND STITCH KEY

☐ With A, k on RS, p on WS

⬜ With B, k on RS, p on WS

⊟ With B, p on RS, k on WS

Sailor Striped Pullover

Ooh-la-la! French-style stripes cover this versatile unisex sweater, perfect for spring and fall.

■■■▫

Sizes
Instructions are written for
size 3 months (6 months, 12 months).
Shown in size 12 months.

Knitted Measurements
Chest 20 (21, 22)"/51 (53.5, 56)cm
Length 10½ (11¼, 12)"/26 (28.5, 30.5)cm
Upper arm 6 (7, 7½)"/15 (16.5, 19)cm

Materials
■ 1 3½oz/100g skein (each approx 240yd/220m) of Cascade Yarns *Cherub Aran* (nylon/acrylic) each in #9 ecru (A), #27 navy (B), and #12 turquoise (C)
■ One pair each sizes 3, 5, and 7 (3.25, 3.75, and 4.5mm) needles *or size to obtain gauge*
■ Stitch holders
■ Snap tape

Stripe Pattern
Working in St st (k on RS, p on WS), work 4 rows A, 4 rows B.
Rep these 8 rows for stripe pat.

Back
With smallest needles and C, cast on 45 (47, 49) sts.
Next row (RS) *K1, p1; rep from * to last st, k1.
K the knit sts and p the purl sts for k1, p1 rib until piece measures 1¼, (1, 1)"/3 (2.5, 2.5)cm from beg, end with a RS row.
Purl 1 row, inc 1 st evenly across—46 (48, 50) sts.

BEGIN STRIPE PAT
Change to largest needles and A.
Work in stripe pat for 28 (32, 36) rows.
Piece measures approx 6 (6½, 7)"/15 (16.5, 18)cm from beg.

SHAPE ARMHOLES
Bind off 3 sts at beg of next 2 rows.
Next (dec) row (RS) SKP, k to last 2 sts, k2tog—2 sts dec'd.
Cont in pat as established, rep dec row every other row twice more—34 (36, 38) sts.
Work even until armhole measures 3½ (3¾, 4)"/9 (9.5, 10)cm, end with a WS row.

SHAPE SHOULDERS
Bind off 4 (4, 3) sts at beg of next 2 rows, then 2 (2, 3) sts at beg of next 4 rows.
Place rem 18 (20, 20) sts on stitch holder for back neck.

Front
Work as for back until armholes measure 2¼ (2½, 2¾)"/5.5 (6.5, 7)cm, end with a RS row.
Place markers to mark the center 10 (12, 12) sts.

SHAPE NECK
Cont in pat as established, p to marker, place next 10 (12, 12) sts on a st holder for front neck, join a 2nd ball of yarn and p to end.
Working both sides at once with separate balls of yarn, cont in pat and dec 1 st at each neck edge every other row 4 times—8 (8, 9) sts rem for each shoulder.
Cont in pat until armhole measures same as back and shape shoulders as for back.

Sleeves
With size 5 (3.75mm) needles and C, cast on 25 (29, 31) sts. Work 6 rows in k1, p1 rib as for back.
Change to largest needles.

BEG STRIPE PAT
Next (inc) row (RS) With A (B, A), knit, inc 3 sts evenly across row—28 (32, 34) sts.
Cont in stripe pat for 5 rows more.

Gauge
18 sts and 24 rows to 4"/10cm over St st using size 7 (4.5mm) needles. *Take time to check gauge.*

Sailor Striped Pullover

SHAPE CAP

Bind off 3 sts at beg of next 2 rows, dec 1 st each side *every* row 3 times, then every *other* row 3 (4, 5) times more—10 (12, 12) sts.
Bind off.

Finishing

Sew right shoulder seam.

NECK TRIM

With RS facing, size 5 (3.75mm) needles, and C, pick up and k 11 sts along left front neck edge, k 10 (12, 12) sts from front neck holder, pick up and k 11 sts along right neck edge, k 18 (20, 20) sts from back neck holder—50 (54, 54) sts. Work 8 rows in k1, p1 rib. Bind off.

SNAP PLACKET

With RS facing, size 5 (3.75mm) needles, and C, pick up and k 13 (13, 14) sts along left front shoulder and neckband. Knit 1 row. Bind off.
With RS facing, size 5 (3.75mm) needles, and C, pick up and k 13 (13, 14) sts along left back shoulder and neckband. Knit 8 rows. Bind off.
Sew snaps to WS of front placket and RS of back placket. Sew outer edge of left front placket to outer edge of back placket, overlapping to the first garter st row of back placket.
Set in sleeves. Sew sleeve and side seams. ■

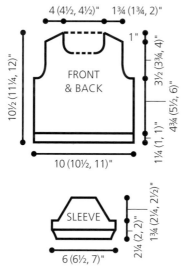

4 (4½, 4½)"   1¾ (1¾, 2)"

1"

10½ (11¼, 12)"

FRONT & BACK

3½ (3¾, 4)"

4¾ (5½, 6)"

1¼ (1, 1)"

10 (10½, 11)"

SLEEVE

1¾ (2¼, 2½)"

2¼ (2, 2)"

6 (6½, 7)"

11

Fair Isle Flakes Sweater

The allover dotted pattern on this pullover adds extra charm
to a traditional snowflake colorwork band.

DESIGNED BY MELISSA LEAPMAN

Sizes
Instructions are written for size
6 months (12 months, 18 months).
Shown in size 6 months

Knitted Measurements
Chest 21 (22, 23)"/53 (56, 58.5)cm
Length 11 (12, 13¼"/28 (30.5, 33.5)cm
Upper arm 9½ (10, 10¾)"/24
(25.5, 27)cm

Materials
■ 2 (2, 3) 1¾oz/50g skeins (each approx
180yd/165m) of Cascade Yarns *Cherub
DK* (nylon/acrylic) in #4 baby pink (A)

■ 1 skein each in #46 burgundy (B),
#26 african violet (C), #29 smokey purple
(D), #53 mauve orchid (E), and #32
cotton candy (F)

■ One pair each sizes 3 and 5
(3.25 and 3.75mm) needles *or size to
obtain gauge*

■ Three ½" (12mm) buttons

■ Stitch holders

K1, P1 Rib
(over an odd number of sts)
Row 1 *K1, p1; rep from *, end k1.
Row 2 K the knit sts and p the purl sts.
Rep row 2 for k1, p1 rib.

Note
Charts are worked in St st (k on RS,
p on WS).

Gauge
25 sts and 28 rows to 4"/10cm over St st and chart pat using larger needles.
Take time to check gauge.

Fair Isle Flakes Sweater

11

Sweater Back

With smaller needles and A, cast on 65 (69, 73) sts. Work in k1, p1 rib for 1"/2.5cm, end with a WS row. Change to larger needles.

BEG BIRD'S EYE CHART

Row 1 (RS) Work to rep line, work 4-st rep 15 (16, 17) times across, work to end of chart. Cont to foll chart in this manner until row 8 is complete. Rep rows 1–8 for 2 (3, 4) times more.

BEG FAIR ISLE CHART

Row 1 (RS) Beg where indicted for size you are making, work to rep line, work 16-st rep 4 times across, work to end for size you are making. Cont to work chart in this manner until row 24 is complete.

BEG BIRD'S EYE CHART

Beg with row 7, work foll Fair Isle chart until piece measures 11 (12, 13¼)"/28 (30.5, 33.5)cm, end with a RS row.
Next row (WS) P20 (21, 22) and place these sts on a st holder, bind off rem sts.

Front

Work as for back until piece measures 9½ (10½, 11¾)"/24 (26.5, 30)cm.

SHAPE NECK

Next row (RS) K22 (23, 24), join a 2nd ball of yarn and bind off center 21 (23, 25) sts, k to end.
Working both sides at once with separate balls of yarn, dec 1 st from each neck edge on next 2 rows—20 (21, 22) sts rem each side.
Work even until piece measures 10¼ (11¼, 12½)"/26 (28.5, 32)cm, end with a WS row.
Next row (RS) Place the first 20 (21, 22) sts on a st holder for left shoulder, work to end on the sts on the right shoulder. Cont on the 20 (21, 22) sts for right shoulder until piece measures same as back. Bind off.

Sleeves

With smaller needles and A, cast on 41 (41, 45) sts. Work in k1, p1 rib for 1"/2.5cm. Change to larger needles.

BEG BIRD'S EYE CHART

Change to larger needles.
Row 1 (RS) Work to rep line, work 4-st rep 9 (9, 10) times across, work to end of chart.
Cont to work chart in this manner, and AT THE SAME TIME, inc 1 st each side every other row 6 (6, 3) times, then every 4th row 3 (5, 8) times—59 (63, 67) sts. Work even until piece measures 6¼ (7, 8¼)"/16 (18, 21)cm. Bind off.

Finishing

Block pieces to finished measurements. Sew right shoulder seam.

NECKBAND

With smaller needles and A, pick up and k 60 (64, 66) sts evenly around neck edge. Work in k1, p1 rib for 1"/2.5cm. Bind off in rib.

BUTTON BAND

From the RS, using smaller needle and A, pick up and k 10 sts for the side of the back neckband, then k20 (21, 22) from back shoulder st holder. Work in k1, p1 rib for 8 rows. Bind off in rib.

BUTTONHOLE BAND

From the RS, using smaller needles, place the 20 (21, 22) sts from front shoulder st holder on needle, then rejoin A and pick up and k 10 sts from the side of the front neckband—30 (31, 32) sts. Beg with k1 on the first WS row, work in k1, p1 rib for 3 rows.
Next (buttonhole) row (RS) Rib 3 (4, 3) sts, [yo, k2tog, rib 6] 3 times, yo, k2tog, rib 1 (1, 3) sts. Cont in rib for 4 rows more. Bind off in rib. Sew on buttons opposite buttonholes.
Place marker 4¾ (5, 5¼)"/12 (12.5, 13.5)cm down from shoulders on front and back. Sew sleeves to armholes between markers, being sure to sew left sleeve through doubled buttonhole and button band thickness. Sew side and sleeve seams. ■

Fair Isle Flakes Sweater

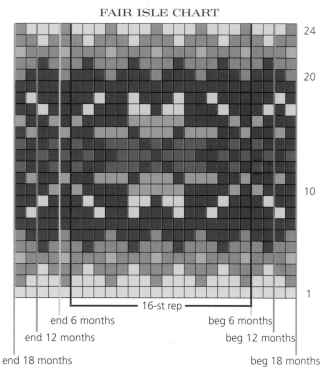

24

20

10

1

16-st rep

end 6 months

end 12 months

end 18 months

beg 6 months

beg 12 months

beg 18 months

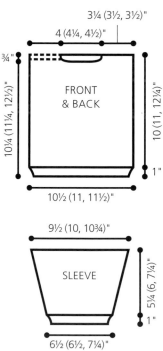

3¼ (3½, 3½)"

4 (4¼, 4½)"

¾"

FRONT & BACK

10¼ (11¼, 12½)"

10 (11, 12¼)"

1"

10½ (11, 11½)"

9½ (10, 10¾)"

SLEEVE

5¼ (6, 7¼)"

1"

6½ (6½, 7¼)"

BIRD'S EYE CHART

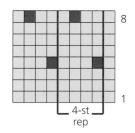

8

1

4-st rep

Gradient Throw

Nine squares are knit diagonally in double garter stitch stripes to form this easy but beautiful ombré blanket.

DESIGNED BY ROSE ANN PENNEY

Knitted Measurements
Approx 26 x 26"/66 x 66cm

Materials
■ 3 3½oz/100g skeins (each approx 240yd/220m) of Cascade Yarns *Cherub Aran Multis* (nylon/acrylic) in #520 tropical sea (MC)

■ 2 3½oz/100g skeins (each approx 240yd/220m) of Cascade Yarns *Cherub Aran* (nylon/acrylic) in #33 peacock (A)

■ 1 skein each in #13 jade (B) and #01 white (C)

■ Size 7 (4.5mm) circular needles, one each 24 and 40"/60 and 100cm long, *or size to obtain gauge*

■ Stitch markers

Double Garter Stitch Stripe Pattern
Row 1 (RS) With MC, knit. Do not turn. Slide work to opposite end of needle to work next row from RS.
Row 2 (RS) With CC, knit. Turn.
Rows 3 and 4 (WS) Rep rows 1 and 2. Rep rows 1–4 for double garter st stripe pat.

Stitch Glossary
kfb Knit into front and back of next st to inc 1 st.

Blanket
SQUARE
(make 3 with A for CC, 3 with B for CC, and 3 with C for CC)
With shorter circular needle and CC, cast on 2 sts.
Next row (RS) K1, kfb—3 sts.
Next (inc) row K1, kfb, k to end—1 st inc'd.
Rep inc row every row 26 times more—30 sts.

BEGIN DOUBLE GARTER ST STRIPE PAT
Cont to rep inc row every row and rep rows 1–4 of double garter st stripe 8 times—62 sts.

BEGIN DECREASE SECTION
Cont in double garter st stripe pat as established, work decs as foll:
Row 1 (dec RS) With MC, k1, [ssk] twice, k to end—2 sts dec'd.

Gauge
20 sts and 40 rows to 4"/10cm over garter st using size 7 (4.5mm) needle.
Take time to check gauge.

Gradient Throw

Row 2 (dec RS) With CC, k1, ssk, k to end—1 st dec'd.
Row 3 (dec WS) With MC, k1, [ssk] twice, k to end—2 sts dec'd.
Row 4 (dec WS) With CC, k1, ssk, k to end—1 st dec'd.
Row 5 (dec RS) With MC, k1, ssk, k to end—1 st dec'd.
Row 6 (dec RS) With CC, k1, ssk, k to end—1 st dec'd.
Row 7 (dec WS) With MC, k1, ssk, k to end—1 st dec'd.
Row 8 (dec WS) With CC, k1, ssk, k to end—1 st dec'd.
Rep rows 1–8 once more, then rows 1–4 once more—36 sts.
Break CC and cont with MC only in garter st.
Row 1 (dec RS) K1, ssk, k to end—1 st dec'd.
Row 2 (dec WS) K1, ssk, k to end—1 st dec'd.
Row 3 (dec RS) K1, [ssk] twice, k to end—2 sts dec'd.
Row 4 (dec WS) K1, ssk, k to end—1 st dec'd.
Row 5 (dec RS) K1, ssk, k to end—1 st dec'd.

Row 6 (dec WS) K1, [ssk] twice, k to end—2 sts dec'd.
Rep rows 1–6 for 3 times more—4 sts.
Next row (RS) K1, ssk, k1.
Next row Sl 1, ssk, psso. Fasten off last st.

Finishing

Sew squares in 3 strips of like colorways. Using photo as guide, sew strips tog.
With longer circular needle, [pick up and k 96 sts evenly along one edge to corner, place marker (pm), pick up and k 3 sts along corner, pm] 3 times, pick up and k 96 sts evenly along one edge to corner, pm, pick up and k 3 sts along corner—396 sts.
Do not join, turn.
Next row (WS) [K to 1 st before marker, kfb, sl marker, k3, sl marker, kfb] 3 times, k to 1 st before marker, kfb, sl marker, k3.
Next row (RS) K3, sl marker, kfb, [k to 1 st before marker, kfb, sl marker, k3, sl marker, kfb] 3 times, k to last st, kfb.
Rep last 2 rows 7 times more. Bind off loosely. ■

13

All About Aran Set

Dress him to impress in a shawl-collar cabled cardigan
and matching pants with textured pockets.

DESIGNED BY GAYLE BUNN

■■■■

Sizes
Instructions are written for size 6 months
(12 months). Shown in size 6 months.

Knitted Measurements
CARDIGAN
Chest (closed) 20 (22)"/51 (56)cm
Length 10½ (11½)"/26.5 (29)cm

PANTS
Waist 18 (20)"/45.5 (51)cm
Hip 20 (22½)"/51 (57)cm
Length 14½ (15½)"/37 (39.5)cm

Materials
■ 2 (3) 3½oz/100g skeins (each
approx 240yd/220m) of Cascade Yarns
Cherub Aran (nylon/acrylic) in #33
peacock (A)

■ 2 skeins in #47 teal (B)

■ One pair each sizes 6 and 7 (4 and
4.5mm) needles *or size to obtain gauge*

■ Cable needle (cn)

■ Stitch holders, stitch markers

■ Three ¹¹⁄₁₆"/17mm buttons

■ ½yd (.5m) of ¾"/19mm elastic

Stitch Glossary
3-st RPC Sl 2 sts to cn and hold to *back,*
k1, p2 from cn.
3-st LPC Sl 1 st to cn and hold to *front,*
p2, k1 from cn.
4-st RC Sl 2 sts to cn and hold to *back,* k2,
k2 from cn.
4-st LC Sl 2 sts to cn and hold to *front,* k2,
k2 from cn.
5-st RPC Sl next 2 sts to cn and hold to
back, k2, p1, k2 from cn.
5-st LPC Sl next 2 sts to cn and hold to
front, k2, p1, k2 from cn.
inc 1 Work p1, k1 in same st.

K1, P1 Rib
(over an odd number of sts)
Row 1 (RS) K1, *p1, k1; rep from * to end.
Row 2 K the knit sts and p the purl sts.
Rep row 2 for k1, p1 rib.

Moss Stitch
(over a multiple of 2 sts plus 1)
Row 1 (RS) K1, *p1, k1; rep from * to end.
Row 2 K the knit sts and p the purl sts.
Row 3 P1, *k1, p1; rep from * to end.
Row 4 K the knit sts and p the purl sts.
Rep rows 1–4 for moss st.

Short Row Wrap & Turn
(w&t)
on RS row (on WS row)

1) Wyib (wyif), sl next st purlwise.
2) Move yarn between the needles to the
front (back).
3) Sl the same st back to LH needle. Turn
work. One st is wrapped.
4) When working the wrapped st, insert
RH needle under the wrap and work it
tog with the corresponding st on needle.

Cardigan Back
With smaller needles and A, cast on 57
(63) sts. Work in k1, p1 rib for 6 rows, inc
11 sts evenly spaced across last row, and
end with a WS row—68 (74) sts. Change
to larger needles.

BEG CHARTS
Row 1 (RS) K3 (6), pm, work chart 1 over
next 17 sts, place marker (pm), [work
chart 2 over next 14 sts] twice, pm, work
chart 3 over next 17 sts, pm, k3 (6).
Keeping 3 (6) sts each side in St st (k on
RS, p on WS), work charts 1 and 3
through row 18, then rep rows 1–18 for
cable pats; work chart 2 through row 4,
then rep rows 1–4 for cable pat. Work
even until piece measures 6¼ (6¾)"/16
(17)cm from beg, end with a WS row.

ARMHOLE SHAPING
Bind off 4 (5) sts at beg of next 2 rows.
Work even on 60 (64) sts until armhole

Gauge
22 sts and 26 rows to 4"/10cm over St st using larger needles. *Take time to check gauge.*

measures 4¼ (4¾)"/11 (12)cm, end with a WS row.

SHOULDER SHAPING
Bind off 17 (18) sts at beg of next 2 rows. Bind off rem 26 (28) sts for back neck in pat.

Left Front
With smaller needles and A, cast on 29 (31) sts. Work in k1, p1 rib for 6 rows, inc 6 (7) sts evenly spaced across last row and end with a WS row—35 (38) sts. Change to larger needles.

BEG CHART PATS
Row 1 (RS) K3 (6), pm, work chart 1 over next 17 sts, pm, work chart 2 over next 14 sts, pm, k1. Keeping 3 (6) sts at beg of row and 1 st at end of row in St st, work chart 1 through row 18, then rep rows 1–18 for cable pat; work chart 2 through row 4, then rep rows 1–4 for cable pat. Work even until piece measures same length as back to underarm, end with a WS row.

ARMHOLE AND NECK SHAPING
Row 1 (dec RS) Bind off 4 (5) sts (armhole), work to last 4 sts, p2tog, k2 (neck edge). Pm at neck edge for front buttonhole band placement.
Row 2 P2, k1, work to end.
Row 3 (dec) Work to last 4 sts, p2tog, k2. Rep last 2 rows 6 (7) times more, end with a RS row—23 (24) sts. Cont to shape neck as foll:
Row 4 (WS) P2, k1, work to end.
Row 5 Work to last 3 sts, p1, k2.
Row 6 Rep row 4.
Row 7 Work to last 4 sts, p2tog, k2. Rep last 4 rows 5 times more. Work even on 17 (18) sts until piece measures same

length as back to shoulder, end with a WS row. Bind off in pat st.

Right Front
With smaller needles and A, cast on 29 (31) sts. Work in k1, p1 rib for 6 rows, inc 6 (7) sts evenly spaced across last row, and end with a WS row—35 (38) sts. Change to larger needles.

BEG CHART PATS
Row 1 (RS) K1, pm, work chart 2 over next 14 sts, pm, work chart 3 over next 17 sts, pm, k3 (6). Keeping 1 st at beg of row and 3 (6) sts at end of row in St st, work chart 1 through row 18, then rep rows 1–18 for cable pat; work chart 2 through row 4, then rep rows 1–4 for cable pat. Work even until piece measures same length as back to underarm, end with a RS row.

ARMHOLE AND NECK SHAPING
Next row (WS) Bind off 4 (5) sts, work to end.

Row 1 (dec RS) K2, p2tog (neck edge), work to end. Pm at neck edge for front button band placement.
Row 2 Work to last 3 sts, k1, p2.
Row 3 (dec) K2, p2tog, work to end. Rep last 2 rows 6 (7) times more, end with a RS row—23 (24) sts. Cont to shape neck as foll:
Row 4 (WS) Work to last 3 sts, k1, p2.
Row 5 K2, p1, work to end.
Row 6 Rep row 4.
Row 7 K2, p2tog, work to end. Rep last 4 rows 5 times more. Work even on 17 (18) sts until piece measures same length as back to shoulder, end with a WS row. Bind off in pat st.

Sleeves
With larger needles and A, cast on 33 (37) sts. Work even in moss st for 8 rows, end with a WS row. Inc 1 st each side on next row, then every 6th row 4 (5) times more, working new sts into pat st. Work even on 43 (49) sts until piece measures 6 (6½)"/15 (16.5)cm. Mark beg and end of last row for beg of sleeve cap. Work even for 4 (5) rows. Bind off in pat st.

Collar
FIRST SIDE
With smaller needles and A, cast on 3 sts.
Row 1 (WS) P1, k1, p1.
Row 2 K1, inc 1 st in next st, k1—4 sts.
Row 3 P2, k1, p1.
Row 4 P1, k1, inc 1 st in next st, k1—5 sts.
Row 5 P2, k1, p1, k1.
Row 6 K1, p1, k1, inc 1 st in next st, k1—6 sts.
Row 7 P2, [k1, p1] twice.
Row 8 [P1, k1] twice, inc 1 st in next st, k1—7 sts.
Row 9 P2, [k1, p1] twice, k1.
Row 10 [K1, p1] twice, k1, inc 1 st in

next st, k1—8 sts.

Row 11 P2, [k1, p1] 3 times.

Cont in moss st as established, cont to inc 1 st at outer edge (as established) on next row, then on every other row twice more, then every 4th row 4 times—15 sts. Place a marker at inner edge of last row to indicate end of inc's. Work even in pat (keeping outer edge st in St st) until piece measures 7½ (8)"/19 (20.5)cm from beg, end with a RS row. Place a marker on inner edge to indicate beg of back neck edge shaping.

BACK NECK EDGE SHAPING

Row 1 (WS) Work as established over first 12 sts; w&t.

Row 2 Work as established over 12 sts.

Row 3 Work as established over first 8 sts; w&t.

Row 4 Work as established over 8 sts.

Row 5 Work as established over first 4 sts; w&t.

Row 6 Work as established over 4 sts. Cont to work even in pat (keeping outer edge st in St st) until piece measures same length as first side from inc edge marker to back neck edge marker, end with a WS row.

SECOND SIDE

Next (dec) row (RS) Work to last 3 sts, p2tog, k1. Rep dec row every 4th row 3 times, then every other row 8 times. Bind off rem 3 sts in pat st.

Finishing

Lightly block pieces to measurements. Sew shoulder seams.

BUTTON BAND

With RS facing, smaller needles, and A, pick up and k 45 (49) sts evenly spaced across right front edge, from bottom

edge to front neck marker. Beg with row 2, work in k1, p1 rib for 7 rows. Bind off loosely in rib.

BUTTONHOLE BAND

With RS facing, smaller needles, and A, pick up and k 45 (49) sts evenly spaced across left front edge from front neck marker to bottom edge. Beg with row 2, work in k1, p1 rib for 3 rows, end with a WS row.

Next (buttonhole) row (RS) Work in rib over first 2 (3) sts, *bind off next 2 sts, work in rib over next 17 (18) sts; rep from * once more, end bind off next 2 sts, work in rib over last 3 sts.

Next row Work in rib, casting on 2 sts over bound-off sts. Work in rib for 2 rows more. Bind off loosely in rib. Sew inner edge of collar to front and back neck edges, butting cast-on and bound-off sts to top edge of button and buttonhole bands. Sew cast-on and bound-off sts to top edge of button and buttonhole bands. Sew top edge of sleeve cap to

straight edge of armhole, then sew side edges of sleeve cap to bound-off sts of armhole. Sew side and sleeve seams. Sew on buttons.

Pants
LEFT LEG

With smaller needles and B, cast on 37 (43) sts. Work in k1, p1 rib for 1½"/4cm, inc 1 st in center of last row and end with a WS row—38 (44) sts. Change to larger needles. Work even in St st (k on RS, p on WS) for 2 rows.

LEG SHAPING

Next (inc) row (RS) K1, M1, knit to last st, M1, k1. Work even for 3 rows. Cont to inc 1 st each side on next row, then every 4th row 7 times more—56 (62) sts. Work even until piece measures 8 (8½)"/20.5 (21.5)cm from beg, end with a WS row. Mark beg and end of last row for beg of crotch.

CROTCH SHAPING

Next (dec) row (RS) K1, k2tog, knit to last 3 sts, ssk, k1—1 sts dec'd. Purl next row. Rep last 2 rows twice more. Work even on 50 (56) sts until piece measures 5½ (6)"/14 (15)cm above marked row, end with a WS row. Beg short row shaping for back as foll:

Row 1 (RS) K35 (38); w&t.

Row 2 P35 (38).

Row 3 K25 (28); w&t.

Row 4 P25 (28).

Row 5 K15 (18); w&t.

Row 6 P15 (18).

Row 7 Knit across all sts, picking up extra wraps. Place sts on holder.

RIGHT LEG

Work as for left leg until piece measures 5½ (6)"/14 (15)cm above marked row, end with a RS row. Beg short row shaping for back as foll:

Row 1 (WS) P35 (38); w&t.
Row 2 K35 (38).
Row 3 P25 (28); w&t.
Row 4 K25 (28).
Row 5 P15 (18); w&t.
Row 6 K15 (18).
Row 7 Purl across all sts, picking up extra wraps. Place sts on holder.

Pockets (make 2)

With larger needles and A, cast on 21 sts. Work even in moss st until piece measures 3¼"/8cm from beg, end with a WS row. Change to B. Knit next row. Bind off all sts knitwise.

Finishing

Lightly block pieces to measurements. Sew a pocket to each leg, positioning it so side edge is 2½ (2¾)"/6.5 (7)cm from front edge and top edge of pocket is 1½ (1¾)"/4 (4.5)cm from top edge of leg. Sew pockets in place. Sew inner leg and crotch seams.

WAISTBAND

With RS facing, circular needle, and B, beg at center back seam, k2tog, k 48 (54) sts from left leg holder, then k2tog, k 48 (54) sts from right leg holder—98 (110) sts. Work around in k1, p1 rib for 2"/5cm. Bind off loosely in rib. Fold waistband in half to WS and sew in place, leaving an opening at center back. Cut elastic to fit waist measurement and draw through waistband. Securely sew ends of elastic together. Sew opening closed. ■

CHART 1

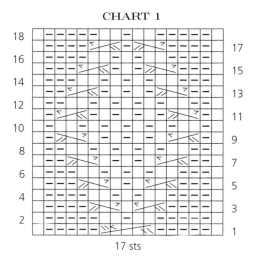

17 sts

CHART 2

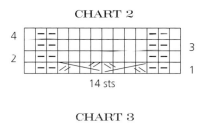

14 sts

CHART 3

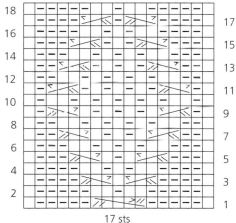

17 sts

STITCH KEY

□ k on RS, p on WS	⧅ 4-st RC
— p on RS, k on WS	⧅ 4-st LC
⧅ 3-st RPC	⧅ 5-st RPC
⧅ 3-st LPC	⧅ 5-st LPC

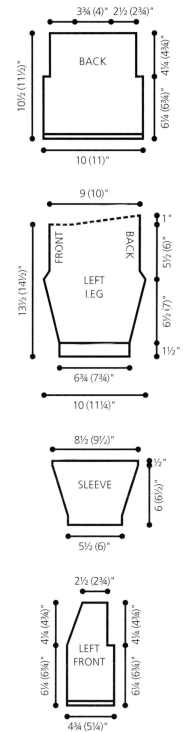

Merry Multis Hat

Use your favorite variegated shade to whip up one (or more!)
of these fun pompom toppers.

DESIGNED BY MATTHEW SCHRANK

Sizes
Instructions are written for size
newborn–6 months.

Knitted Measurements
Circumference (unstretched)
11½"/29cm
Length 6½"/16.5cm

Materials
■ 1 1¾oz/50g skein (each approx
180yd/165m) of Cascade Yarns
Cherub DK Multis (nylon/acrylic) each in
#511 carnival (MC), OR 505 rainbow
brights (MC), OR #522 spring (MC)

■ 1 1¾oz/50g skein (each approx
180yd/165m) of Cascade Yarns *Cherub
DK* (nylon/acrylic) in #09 ecru (CC)

■ One set (5) size 4 (3.5mm)
double-pointed needles (dpns) *or size to
obtain gauge*

■ Stitch marker

Hat
With CC, cast on 80 sts. Join, being
careful not to twist sts, and place marker
for beg of rnd.
Next rnd *K1, p1; rep from * around.

Cont in k1, p1 rib for 1"/2.5cm. Break CC.
With MC, work in St st (k every rnd) until
piece measures 5½"/14cm from beg.

SHAPE CROWN
Next (dec) rnd [K8, k2tog] 8 times
around—72 sts.
Next (dec) rnd [K7, k2tog] 8 times
around—64 sts.
Cont to dec in this way, working
1 less st before the k2tog every rnd until
16 sts rem.
Next (dec) rnd [K2tog] 8 times around.
Break yarn, leaving a long tail. Thread tail
through rem 8 sts and pull tight to close.

Finishing
With CC, make a 2"/5cm pompom and
fasten to top of hat. ■

Pattern for
Geometric Rattles
is on page 69.

Gauge
28 sts and 36 rnds to 4"/10cm over St st using size 4 (3.5mm) needles. *Take time to check gauge.*

Violet Vest

With its layer-friendly shape and textured stitch pattern, this vest
is the perfect way to show off multicolor yarn.

DESIGNED BY BROOKE NICO

Sizes
Instructions are written for size
newborn–3 months (6–12 months).
Shown in size newborn–3 months.

Chest (closed) 17 (21)"/43 (53)cm
Length 9½ (11)"/24 (28)cm

Materials
■ 2 1¾oz/50g skeins (each approx
180yd/165m) of Cascade Yarns
Cherub DK (nylon/acrylic) in #508
pink/purple print

■ One each sizes 3 and 5 (3.25 and
3.75mm) circular needles, 24"/60cm
long, *or size to obtain gauge*

■ Four ⅝" (15mm) buttons

Stitch Glossary
Inc 1 Work (p1 and k1) into next st.

7x1 Mock Cable Rib
(multiple of 8 sts plus 1, plus garter
bands)
Note For the gauge swatch
(incorporating the 4-st garter borders),
using larger needles, cast on 33 sts.
Row 1 (RS) K4, *p1, k1, [sl 1, k1, yo,
psso the k1 and yo or the 2 previous sts]
3 times; rep from * to last 5 sts, p1, k4.
Row 2 K5, *p7, k1; rep from *, end k4.
Row 3 K4, *p1, [sl 1, k1, yo, psso the 2
previous sts] 3 times, k1; rep from * to
last 5 sts, p1, k4.
Row 4 Rep row 2.
Rep rows 1–4 for 7x1 mock cable rib
with a 4-st garter band at each edge.

Vest
With smaller needle, cast on 81 (93) sts.
Row 1 (RS) K4, *p1, k2; rep from *, end
last rep k4 instead of k2.
Row 2 K5, *p2, k1; rep from * to last 4
sts, end k4.
Buttonhole row 3 K4, *p1, k2; rep from
* to last 5 sts, end p1, k1, yo, k2tog (for
buttonhole), k1.
Row 4 Rep row 2.
Change to larger needles.
Row 5 (inc) K4, *inc 1 (see stitch
glossary), k2; rep from * to last 5 sts, end
p1, k4—105 (121) sts.
Rows 6, 8, and 10 K5, p3, k1; rep
from *, end k4.

Row 7 K4, *p1, sl 1, k1, yo, psso
(the 2 previous sts), k1; rep from *,
end p1, k4.
Row 9 K4, *p1, k1, sl 1, k1, yo, psso;
rep from *, end p1, k4.
Row 11 (inc) K4, *inc 1, sl 1, k1, yo,
psso, k1; rep from *, end p1, k4—129
(149) sts.
Rows 12, 14, 16, 18, and 20 K5, *p4,
k1; rep from *, end k4.
Buttonhole row 13 K4, *p1, [sl 1, k1,
yo, psso] twice; rep from * to the last
5 sts, end p1, k1, yo, k2tog (for
buttonhole), k1.
Row 15 K4, *p1, k1, sl 1, k1, yo, psso,
k1; rep from *, end p1, k4.
Row 17 K4, *p1, [sl 1, k1, yo, psso]
twice; rep from *, end p1, k4.
Row 19 Rep row 15.
Row 21 (inc) K4, *inc 1, [sl 1, k1, yo,
psso] twice; rep from * to last 5 sts, end
p1, k4—153 (177) sts.
Rows 22, 24, 26, 28, and 30 K5, *p5,
k1; rep from *, end k4.
Buttonhole row 23 K4, *p1, [sl 1, k1,
yo, psso] twice, k1; rep from * to last 5
sts, end p1, k1, yo, k2tog (for
buttonhole), k1.
Row 25 K4, *p1, k1, [sl 1, k1, yo, psso]
twice; rep from *, end p1, k4.
Row 27 K4, *p1, [sl 1, k1, yo, psso]
twice, k1; rep from *, end p1, k4.
Row 29 Rep row 25.

Gauge
26 sts and 32 rows to 4"/10cm after blocking over 7x1 mock cable rib using larger needle. *Take time to check gauge.*

Violet Vest

15

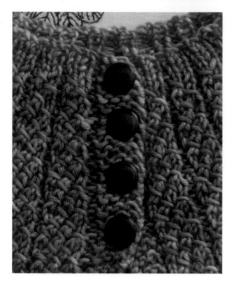

Inc row 31 K4, *inc 1, [sl 1, k1, yo, psso] twice, k1; rep from *, end p1, k4—177 (205) sts.

Rows 32, 34, 36, 38, and 40 K5, *p6, k1, rep from *, end k4.

Buttonhole row 33 K4, *p1, [sl 1, k1, yo, psso] 3 times; rep from *, end p1, k1, yo, k2tog (for buttonhole), k1.

Row 35 K4, *p1, k1, [sl 1, k1, yo, psso] twice, k1; rep from *, end p1, k4.

Row 37 K4, *p1, [sl 1, k1, yo, psso] 3 times; rep from *, end p1, k4.

Row 39 Rep row 35.

COMPLETE SLEEVES

Row 41 K4, p1, *[sl 1, k1, yo, psso] 3 times, p1*; rep from * to * 2 (3) times more, then bind off the next 41 sts for sleeve, rep from * to * 6 (8) times, then bind off the next 41 sts for sleeve, rep from * to * 3 (4) times, k4.

Row 42 (WS) K5, [p6, k1] 3 (4) times, cast on 13 sts for body, k1, [p6, k1] 6 (8) times, cast on 13 sts for body, k1, [p6, k1] 3 (4) times, k4—121 (149) sts.

BODY

Row 43 Rep row 35.

Row 44 Rep row 32.

Row 45 (inc) K4, *inc 1, [sl 1, k1, yo, psso] 3 times; rep from *, end p1, k4—137 (169) sts. Then, beg with row 2, work in 7x1 mock cable rib as now established until piece measures 5 (6½)"/12.5 (16.5)cm from armhole cast-on. Bind off in pat.

Finishing

Block pieces to measurements.
Sew on buttons. ∎

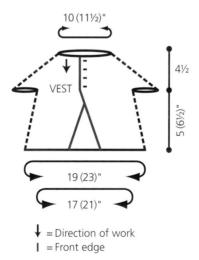

10 (11½)"

4½

5 (6½)"

VEST

19 (23)"

17 (21)"

↓ = Direction of work
| = Front edge

Unicorn Pillow

Who says unicorns don't exist? A comfy pillow doubles as a fantastical friend, with a horn, fuzzy mane and tail, and striped legs.

DESIGNED BY AMY BAHRT

Knitted Measurements
Approx 12 x 16"/30 5 x 40cm

Materials
- 2 3½oz/100g skeins (each approx 240yd/220m) of Cascade Yarns *Cherub Aran* (nylon/acrylic) in #32 cotton candy (A)
- 1 skein in #15 orchid (B)
- 1 3½oz/100g skein (each approx 240yd/220m) of Cascade Yarns *Cherub Aran Sparkle* (nylon/acrylic/metallic) in #201 white (C)
- One pair size 7 (4.5mm) needles *or size to obtain gauge*
- Size G/6 (4mm) crochet hook
- Approx 12"/30.5cm of ½"/1.5cm floral embroidered trim (optional)
- 12 x 16"/30.5 x 40.5cm pillow form
- Small amount of fiberfill
- Two ½"/12mm flat 4-hole white buttons
- Sewing needle and gray thread

Stitch Glossary
spp Sl 1, purl 1, psso to dec 1 st.

Stripe Pattern
In St st, work 2 rows A, 2 rows B. Rep these 4 rows for stripe pat.

Pillow
With A, cast on 116 sts. Work in St st (k on RS, p on WS) for 16"/40.5cm. Bind off.

Legs (make 4)
With B, cast on 15 sts. Work in garter st (k every row) for 1¼"/3cm. Join A and work in stripe pat until piece measures 6½"/16.5cm from beg. Bind off.

Head (make 2)
With A, cast on 16 sts.
Work in St st, foll chart through row 59 for shaping and color change. Bind off.

Ears (make 2)
With A, cast on 3 sts. Work in St st for 2 rows. Inc 1 st each side every other row twice—7 sts. Work 6 rows even. Dec 1 st each side every other row twice—3 sts. Break yarn and thread tail through rem sts. Pull tightly to close and tack securely.

Horn
With A, cast on 14 sts. Work 4 rows in St st. Cont in stripe pat and dec 1 st each side every 4th row 5 times. Purl 1 (WS) row. Break yarn and thread tail through rem 4 sts. Sew seam.

Gauge
18 sts and 26 rows to 4"/10cm over St st using size 7 (4.5mm) needles. *Take time to check gauge.*

Unicorn Pillow

Finishing

Fold legs in half lengthwise. Sew seam, leaving bound-off edge open. Stuff lightly. Sew closed.

Sew head pieces tog with RS tog, leaving bound-off edge open. Stuff to desired size. Sew closed.

Stuff horn to form stiff cone shape. Sew closed. Sew floral trim around base of horn. Sew horn to head approx 1½"/4cm from neck edge (see chart). Embroider chain st around ears and sew ears and eyes to head, foll chart for placement.

Fold body piece in half widthwise. Sew back edge. Place head at top of fold and sew front edge through all layers of fabric. Place pillow in body. Arrange legs along lower edge of body, using photo as guide, sew body closed through all layers.

TAIL

Cut 18 strands of C, each 17"/43cm long. Fold in half and tie tog at top of fold. Sew to top corner opposite head. Sew trim around base of tail.

MANE

Cut 100 strands of C, each 10"/25.5cm long. Holding 2 strands tog, fold in half. With crochet hook, draw loop through a stitch along the spine of the unicorn halfway to the head. Pull the ends of the strands through the loop and tighten. Rep along the spine and neck to the horn and in front of the horn between the ears. Trim mane to 4"/10cm. ■

COLOR AND STITCH KEY

▢	A
◼	B
◹	k2tog on RS, p2tog on WS
◺	SKP on RS, spp on WS
Ⴘ	kfb
●	eye placement
✖	horn placement
⬮	ear placement

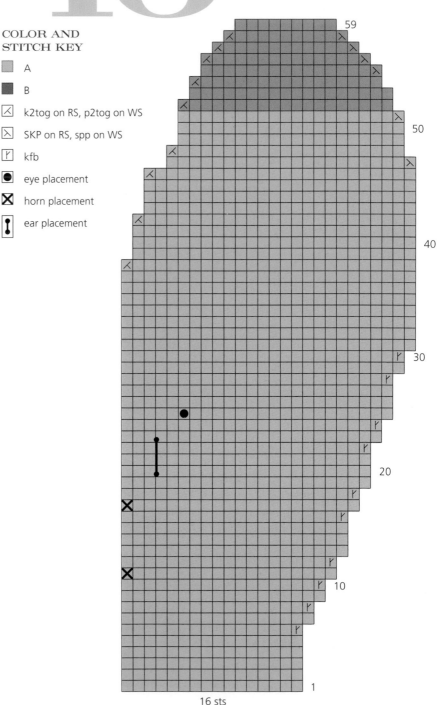

16 sts

Bobble & Bow Booties

Itty-bitty bobbles, picot edges, and a dainty ribbon add a touch
of girly charm to a basic bootie shape.

DESIGNED BY ROSEMARY DRYSDALE

Size
Instructions are written for one size, to fit
3–6 months.

Knitted Measurements
Ankle circumference 5"/12.5cm
Length from heel to toe 3¾"/9.5cm

Materials
■ 1 1¾oz/50g skein (each approx
180yd/165m) of Cascade Yarns *Cherub
DK* (nylon/acrylic) in #53 mauve orchid

■ One pair size 4 (3.5mm) needles *or size
to obtain gauge*

■ 40"/101.5cm lavender ribbon (for tie)

Stitch Glossary
Make bobble (MB) [K1, yo] twice in
same st, turn, p4, turn, [k2tog] twice,
pass first st over 2nd st.

Booties
Cast on 31 sts. Purl 1 (WS) row.
Row 1 (RS) [K1, kfb, k12, kfb] twice,
k1—35 sts.
Row 2 and all WS rows Purl.
Row 3 [K1, kfb, k14, kfb] twice,
k1—39 sts.
Row 5 [K1, kfb, k16, kfb] twice,
k1—43 sts.
Row 7 [K1, kfb, k18, kfb] twice,
k1—47 sts.
Work 2 rows even in St st (k on RS,
p on WS).
Next row (RS) K2tog tbl, k to last 2 sts,
k2tog—45 sts.
Purl 1 row.

INSTEP
Row 1 (RS) K27, k2tog tbl, turn.
Row 2 Sl 1, p9, p2tog, turn.
Row 3 Sl 1, k9, k2tog tbl, turn.
Row 4 Rep row 2.
Row 5 Sl 1, k4, MB, k4, k2tog tbl, turn.
Rep rows 2–5 twice more, then row 2
once—31 sts, 10 sts on each side of 11
instep sts.
Next row (RS) Sl 1, k20, turn.
Next row P to end.
Work 2 rows even in St st.

LEG
Eyelet row (RS) *K1, yo, k2tog; rep
from * to last st, k1.
Work 3 rows in St st.
Next row (RS) *K1, p1; rep from *
to last st, k1.
K the knit sts and p the purl sts for k1,
p1 rib for 11 rows more.
Next (turning) row (RS) Knit.

CUFF
Note that the RS of the bootie is the
WS of the cuff.
Next (cuff) row (RS) Knit.
Cont in St st as established for 5
rows more.
Next (bobble) row (RS) [K3, MB] 7
times, k3.
Work 4 rows in St st.
Picot row (WS) P1, *p2tog, yo; rep
from *, end p2.
Knit 1 row. Bind off purlwise.

Finishing
Fold in half and sew seam from turning
row to toe. Fold hem at picot row and
sew down. Fold cuff to RS at turning row.

TIES
Cut ribbon in half to make 2 ties. Thread
through eyelets and tie in bow. ■

Gauge
24 sts and 32 rows/rnds to 4"/10cm over St st using size 4 (3.5mm) needles. *Take time to check gauge.*

18

Duckie Delights Blanket

A happy scene unfolds when you unfold this blanket: two landlubber ducks watch as the rest swim with life preservers!

DESIGNED BY AMY BAHRT

Knitted Measurements
Approx 30½ x 32½"/77.5 x 82.5cm

Materials
■ 3 3½oz/100g skeins (each approx 240yd/220m) of Cascade Yarns *Cherub Aran* (nylon/acrylic) in #21 grass (A)

■ Two skeins in #13 jade (B)

■ One skein each in #19 geranium (C), #43 goldenrod (D), #36 cactus (E), and #01 white (F)

■ Size 7 (4.5mm) circular needle, 32"/80cm long, *or size to obtain gauge*

■ One set (2) size 7 (4.5mm) double-pointed needles (dpns)

■ Embroidery needle

Notes
1) Blanket is worked in rows. Circular needle is used to accommodate large number of sts. Do not join.
2) Color work is done using the intarsia method. Use separate bobbins or lengths of yarn for each color section. Do not carry colors across WS of work.
3) When changing colors, twist strands on WS to prevent holes in work.

Blanket
With A and circular needle, cast on 138 sts. Work 11 rows in garter st.
Next row (WS) Cont in garter st over 5 sts, place marker (pm), p to last 5 sts, pm, work in garter st to end.
Next row (RS) With A, work in garter st to marker, sl marker, with B, k2; with a 2nd ball of A, k to end.
Next row Working colors as they appear, work in garter st to marker, sl marker, work in St st to next marker, sl marker, work in garter st to end.
Rep last 2 rows once more.

Note Read before cont to knit: charts are worked AT THE SAME TIME as the color shift pats.

BEGIN COLOR SHIFT PAT 1
Cont in this way, working in garter st outside of markers and St st for center of blanket, work in color shift pat as foll:
Next row With A, work to marker, sl marker, k4 B, with A, work to end.
Next row Work colors as they appear. Cont in this manner, work 2 more sts in B (and 2 fewer sts in A) every other row 6 times more for color shift pat 1.
Next row (WS) Work colors as they appear.

BEGIN COLOR SHIFT PAT 2 AND CHART 1
Cont as established, *only* working 1 st more in B (and 1 less st in A) every other row 86 times. AT THE SAME TIME, when 18 rows have been worked above the garter st border, beg chart 1.
Next row (RS) Work to marker, work 41 sts in color shift pat, work chart 1 over 18 sts, work in pat to end. Cont in pats until row 27 of chart 1 is complete. Work 4 rows in color shift pat 2.

Gauge
18 sts and 26 rows to 4"/10cm over St st using size 7 (4.5mm) needles.
Take time to check gauge.

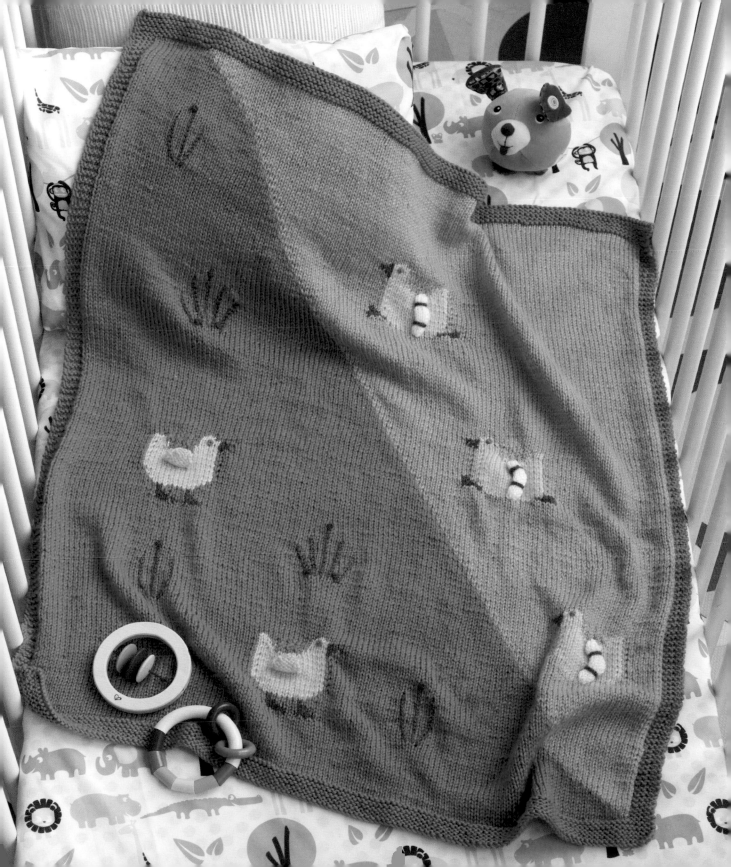

Duckie Delights Blanket

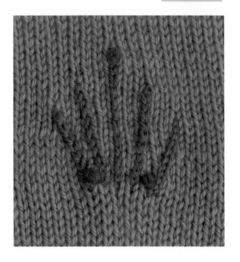

CHART 2
Next row (RS) Work to marker,
sl marker, work 8 sts in color shift pat 2,
work chart 2 over next 18 sts, work in
pat to end.
Cont in pats until row 22 is complete.
Work 5 rows in color shift pat 2.

CHART 1
Next row (RS) Work to marker, sl marker,
work 92 sts in color shift pat, work chart
1 over 18 sts, work in pat to end.
Cont in pats until row 27 of chart 1
is complete. Work 4 rows in color shift
pat 2.

CHART 3
Next row (RS) Work to marker, sl marker,
work 26 sts in color shift pat, work chart
3 over 21 sts, work in pat to end.
Cont in pats until row 22 of chart 3 is
complete. Work 31 rows in color shift
pat 2.

CHART 3
Next row (RS) Work to marker, work
47 sts in color shift pat 2, work chart 3
over 21 sts, work to end.
Cont in pats until row 22 of chart 3
is complete.
When color shift pat 2 is complete,
work color shift pat 1 for 14 rows.
Break B.
With A, work 10 rows in garter st.
Bind off.

Finishing
With embroidery needle and strand
of A, work French knots for duck eyes
as indicated on charts.

DUCK WINGS (MAKE 2)
With D, cast on 8 sts. Work 4 rows in St
st. Dec 1 st each side every other row 3
times—2 sts. K2tog, fasten off. Sew
wing to duck as indicated in chart 1.

LIFE PRESERVERS (MAKE 3)
With F and dpn, cast on 6 sts, *k6,
slide sts to opposite end of needle to
work next row from RS, pulling yarn
tightly across back of work; rep from *
for I-cord until cord measures
2½"/5.5cm from beg.
With crochet hook and C, make a
3"/7.5cm chain and wrap around life
preserver twice, and tack at back, using
photo as guide. Sew life preservers to
swimming ducks as indicated in charts.

GRASS AND BERRIES
Using photo as guide, embroider
grass and berries with strands of E and
chain st for grass, and French knots in
C for berries. ■

CHART 2

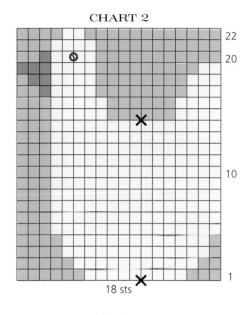

18 sts

CHART 3

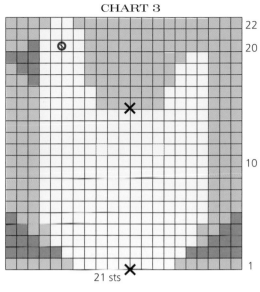

21 sts

CHART 1

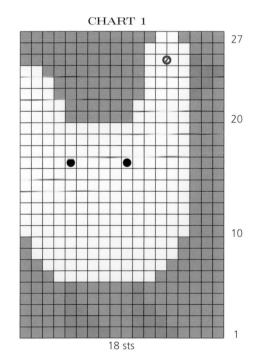

18 sts

COLOR AND STITCH KEY

▨	A
▨	B
☐	C
▨	D
⊘	French knot
●	wing placement
☒	life preserver placement

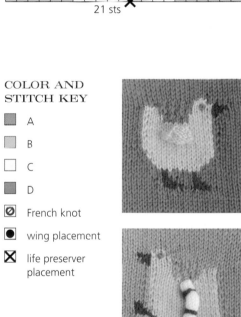

19

Textured Leg Warmers

Over leggings or under a dress, these snug cable-and-eyelet
leg warmers make any outfit winter-ready.

DESIGNED BY BARB BROWN

Size
Instructions are written for one size.

Knitted Measurements
Circumference (unstretched) 5½"/14cm
Length 6½"/16.5cm

Materials
■ 1 1¾oz/50g skein (each approx
180yd/165m) of Cascade Yarns
Cherub DK (nylon/acrylic) in #15 orchid

■ One set size 3 (3.25mm)
double-pointed needles (dpns) *or size
to obtain gauge*

■ Stitch marker

Pattern Stitch
(multiple of 3 sts)
Rnd 1 *K2, p1; rep from * around.
Rnd 2 *K1, yo, k1, p1; rep from
* around.
Rnd 3 *K3, p1; rep from * around.

Rnd 4 *Sl 1, k2, pass the sl st over 2 sts,
p1; rep from * around.
Rep rnds 1–4 for pat st.

Leg Warmer
Cast on 51 sts. Place marker and join,
being careful not to twist sts.
Work in pat st until piece measures
6½"/16.5cm or desired length from beg,
end with a rnd 4.
Bind off loosely in pat. ■

Gauge
36 sts and 38 rnds to 4"/10cm over pat st unstretched using size 3 (3.25mm) needles.
Take time to check gauge.

Slip Stitch Henley

A simple shape and textured stitch pattern show off variegated colors, and a sporty henley neckline allows for easy on-and-off.

DESIGNED BY DEBBIE O'NEILL

Sizes
Instructions are written for size 3 months (6 months, 12 months). Shown in size 6 months.

Knitted Measurements
Chest 18½ (20½, 22½)"/47 (52, 57)cm
Length (9¾, 10¾, 11¾)"/24.5 (27, 30)cm
Upper arm 7¾ (8, 8½)"/20 (20.5, 21.5)cm

Materials
■ 2 (3, 3) 1¾oz/50g skeins (each approx 180yd/165m) of Cascade Yarns *Cherub DK* (nylon/acrylic) in #515 daffodil
■ One pair size 3 (3.25mm) needles *or size to obtain gauge*
■ Size 3 (3.25mm) circular needle, 16"/41cm long
■ 4 stitch holders

Stitch Glossary
Little wing st Insert RH needle knitwise in next st and under the 3 strands in the 3 rows below—4 strands on needle, knit the strands as 1 st.

3-Needle Bind-Off
1) Hold right sides of pieces together on 2 needles. Insert 3rd needle knitwise into first st of each needle, and wrap yarn knitwise.
2) Knit these 2 sts together, and slip them off the needles. *Knit the next 2 sts together in the same manner.
3) Slip first st on 3rd needle over 2nd st and off needle. Rep from * in step 2 across row until all sts are bound off.

Pullover Back
With straight needles, cast on 55 (61, 67) sts. Knit 6 rows. Purl 1 row.

BEG CHART
Chart row 1 (RS) Beg where indicated for size, work to rep line, work 10-st rep 4 (4, 6) times, work to end where indicated for size.
Cont to work chart in this manner until row 12 is complete, rep rows 1–12 twice more, then rows 1–4 once. Work in St st until piece measures 9½ (10½, 11½)"/24 (26.5, 29)cm, end with a WS row.

SHAPE NECK
Next row (RS) K14 (17, 20), bind off center 27 sts, k to end. Place rem sts on holders for shoulders.

Front
Cast on and work as for back until the front measures 5¾ (6¾, 7¼)"/14.5 (17, 18.5)cm, end with a WS row.

LEFT FRONT PLACKET OPENING
Next row (RS) K 26 (29, 32) sts for left front, cast on 3 sts for placket—29 (32, 35) sts. Place rem 29 (32, 35) sts on holder to be worked later. Turn work.
Next row (WS) K3, purl to end.
Next row (RS) Knit. Rep last 2 rows until placket opening measures 2¼"/5.5cm, end with a RS row.
Next row (WS) Bind off 7 sts, purl to end—22 (25, 28) sts.
Cont in St st and bind off at neck edge (beg WS rows) 3 sts once, 2 sts twice, 1 st once—14 (17, 20) sts.
Work even until same length as back, end with a RS row. Place sts on holder.

RIGHT FRONT PLACKET OPENING
Sl sts to needle, ready for RS row.
Next row (RS) Knit.
Next row (WS) Purl to last 3 sts, k3. Rep last 2 rows until placket opening measures 2¼"/5.5cm, end with a WS row.

Gauge
24 sts and 32 rows to 4"/10cm after blocking over chart pattern using size 3 (3.25mm) needles.
Take time to check gauge.

20

Slip Stitch Henley

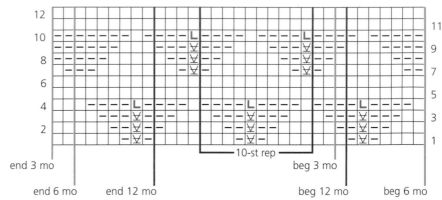

end 3 mo   end 6 mo   end 12 mo   10-st rep   beg 3 mo   beg 12 mo   beg 6 mo

STITCH KEY

☐ k on RS, p on WS   ⊟ p on RS, k on WS   ☒ slip 1 wyif   🄻 little wing

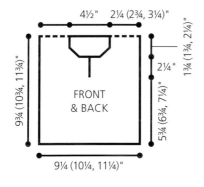

FRONT & BACK

4½"   2¼ (2¾, 3¼)"

9¾ (10¾, 11¾)"   1¾ (1¾, 2¼)"   2¼"   5¾ (6¾, 7¼)"

9¼ (10¼, 11¼)"

SLEEVE

7¾ (8, 8½)"

6 (6½, 7)"

5¼ (5½, 6)"

Next row (RS) Bind off 7 sts, knit to end—22 (25, 28) sts. Cont in St st and bind off at beg of RS rows same as for left front—14 (17, 20) sts.
Work even until same length as back, end with a WS row. Place sts on holder.

Sleeves

Cast on 32 (34, 36) sts. Knit 6 rows. Work 2 rows St st.
Inc row (RS) K1, M1, knit to last st, M1, k1—2 sts inc'd.
Cont in St st, rep inc row every 6th row 6 (6, 7) more times—46 (48, 52) sts.
Work even until sleeve measures 6 (6½, 7)"/15.5(16.5, 18)cm. Bind off loosely.

Finishing

Place right front sts on needle ready for a RS row, and right back sts on a 2nd needle. With RS tog and spare needle, beg at neck edge and join the right shoulder seam using the 3-needle bind-off method.

Place left front sts on needle ready for a WS row, and left back sts on a 2nd needle. With RS tog, beg at neck edge and join the shoulder seam using the 3-needle bind-off method. Center sleeve tops at shoulder seam, sew sleeves in place. Match pattern at sides, sew sleeve and side seams. Sew cast-on end of left placket to first row of right placket.

COLLAR

With RS facing and circular needle, pick up and k 70 sts evenly around neck opening, including top edge of plackets. Knit 4 rows. Bind off loosely.
Block gently to measurements. ■

Hugs & Hearts Onesie

A panel of hearts down the center is the highlight of a textured romper with leg snaps and a back neck opening.

DESIGNED BY LINDA CYR

■■■■

Sizes

Instructions are written for size 6 months (12 months, 18 months, 24 months). Shown in size 6 months.

Knitted Measurements

Chest 20 (22, 23, 24½)"/56 (58.5, 60, 62)cm
Length 19¼ (24¼, 27¼, 30¼)"/49 (61.5, 69, 77)cm
Upper arm 7 (8, 8½, 9½)"/18 (20.5, 21.5, 24)cm

Materials

■ 4 (6, 7, 8) 1¾oz/50g skeins (each approx 180yd/165m) of Cascade Yarns *Cherub DK* (nylon/acrylic) in #8 baby blue

■ One pair each sizes 2 and 4 (2.75 and 3.5mm) needles *or size to obtain gauge*

■ Cable needle (cn)

■ Three ½"/13mm shank buttons

■ Snap tape

■ Stitch holder

■ Size E/4 (3.5mm) crochet hook

K1, P1 Rib

(over an odd number of sts)
Row 1 (RS) *K1, p1; rep from * to last st, k1.
Row 2 K the knit sts and p the purl sts.
Rep row 2 for k1, p1 rib.

Moss Stitch

Row 1 (RS) *K1, p1; rep from * to end.
Rows 2 and 4 K the knit sts and p the purl sts.
Row 3 *P1, k1; rep from * to end.
Rep rows 1–4 for moss st.

Stitch Glossary

4-st RC Sl 2 to cn and hold to *back,* k2, k2 from cn.
4-st LC Sl 2 to cn and hold to *front,* k2, k2 from cn.
2-st RC Sl 1 to cn and hold to *back,* k1, k1 from cn.
2-st LC Sl 1 to cn and hold to *front,* k1, k1 from cn.
1/2 RPC Sl 1 to cn and hold to *back,* k2, p1 from cn.
1/2 LPC Sl 1 to cn and hold to *front,* k2, p1 from cn.
2/1 LPC Sl 2 to cn and hold to *front,* p1, k2 from cn.

Cable Panel

(over 22 sts)
Rows 1, 5, 9, and 13 P1, k4, p2, k8, p2, k4, p1.
Row 2 and all WS rows K the knit sts and p the purl sts.
Rows 3 and 15 P1, 4-st RC, p2, 4-st RC, 4-st LC, p2, 4-st LC, p1.
Rows 7 and 11 P1, 4-st RC, p2, 4-st LC, 4-st RC, p2, 4-st LC, p1.
Row 16 Rep row 2.
Rep rows 1–16 for cable panel.

Gauge

34 sts and 40 rows to 4"/10cm over moss st using larger needles. *Take time to check gauge.*

Hugs & Hearts Onesie

Heart Panel
(over 14 sts)
Row 1 (RS) P6, k2, p6.
Rows 2, 4, 6, 8, 10, and 12 K the knit sts and p the purl sts.
Row 3 P5, 2-st RC, 2-st LC, p5.
Row 5 P4, 1/2 RPC, 2/1 LPC, p4.
Row 7 P3, 1/2 RPC, p2, 2/1 LPC, p3.
Row 9 P2, 1/2 RPC, p4, 2/1 LPC, p2.
Row 11 [P2, k2] 3 times, p2.
Row 13 P2, 2/1 LPC, sl 1 to cn, hold in back, k1, p1 from cn, sl 1 to cn, hold in front, p1, k1 from cn, 1/2 RPC, p2.
Row 14 K3, yo, sl 2 purlwise, insert tip of LH needle into first slipped st and pass over 2nd st, replace st on LH needle, insert tip of RH needle into 2nd st on LH needle purlwise, pass over first st, k first st, yo, k2, yo, sl 1 purlwise, insert tip of RH needle purlwise into 2nd st on LH needle, pass over first st, sl onto RH needle, insert tip of LH needle into 2nd st from the end of RH needle, pass over first st, replace onto LH needle, k1, yo, k3.
Row 15 P to end.
Row 16 Rep row 2.
Rep rows 1–16 for heart panel.

Right Cable
(over 5 sts)
Rows 1 and 5 (RS) P1, k4.
Rows 2, 4, and 6 K the knit sts and p the purl sts.
Row 3 P1, 4-st RC.
Rep rows 1–6 for right cable.

Romper Front
LEFT LEG
With smaller needles, cast on 31 (35, 37, 39) sts. Work in k1, p1 rib for 1"/2.5cm, inc 8 (8, 10, 12) sts across last row—39 (43, 47, 51) sts. Change to larger needles.

BEGIN PATTERNS
Next row (RS) K1 (selvage st), work 10 (14, 17, 19) sts in moss st, work 22 sts of cable panel, work 5 (5, 6, 8) sts in moss st, k1 (selvage st).
Cont in pats as established for 3 (7, 7, 7) rows.
Note Read before cont to knit.
Next (inc) row (RS) Work to last st, M1, k1.
Cont to inc 1 st inside selvage st at end of RS rows, every 4th row 7 (9, 10 12) times more, every other row 4 (4, 4, 2) times, working incs into pats, so that final pat set-up is as foll:
(RS) K1, 10 (14, 17, 19) sts moss st, 22 sts cable panel, 6 (8, 10, 12) sts moss st, 5 sts right cable, p6, k1—51 (57, 62, 66) sts. Place sts on holder.

RIGHT LEG
Work as for left leg, reversing all shaping and pat placement. Work left cable instead of right cable at shaped edge.

BODY
Next row (RS) Place left leg sts on needle with right leg sts—102 (114, 122, 132) sts.
Cont as established, working center 2 sts as p2, for 2 rows. Work center 14 sts in heart panel and rem sts as established until piece measures 2¾ (3¼, 2, 2)"/7 (8, 5, 5)cm above leg joining.

SHAPE SIDES
Dec 1 st at each side inside selvage sts on next row, then every 8th row 6 (7, 9, 11) times more—88 (98, 102, 108) sts. Work even until piece measures 8¾ (11¾, 13½, 15)"/22.5 (30, 33.5, 38)cm above leg joining.

SHAPE ARMHOLE
Bind off 3 sts at beg of next 2 rows. Work 2 rows even. Dec 1 st at each side of next row—80 (90, 94, 100) sts. Work even until armhole measures 3¼ (3¾, 4¼, 4¾)"/8 (9.5, 10.5, 12)cm.

SHAPE NECK
Next row (RS) Work 33 (38, 40, 43) sts, join 2nd ball of yarn and bind off center 14 sts, work to end. Working both sides at once with separate balls of yarn, bind off from each neck edge 4 sts 1 (2, 2, 2) times, 3 sts once, 2 sts 2 (1, 2, 3) times—22 (25, 25, 26) sts each side. Work even until armhole measures 4½ (5, 5½, 6)"/11 (12.5, 14, 15)cm, end with a RS row.

SHAPE SHOULDERS
Bind off from each shoulder edge 8 (9, 9, 10) sts once, 7 (8, 8, 8) sts twice.

Back
Work as for front until piece measures 9¾ (13½, 15¼, 17¼)"/24 (34, 38, 43)cm above leg joining.

Hugs & Hearts Onesie

PLACKET

Next row (RS) Work 33 (38, 40, 43) sts in pat, p5, k2, join 2nd ball of yarn and p2, k5, work to end.
Work both sides at once and shape as for front. Work even until same length as front to shape shoulder.

SHAPE NECK AND SHOULDER

Shape shoulders as for front, AT THE SAME TIME, bind off from each neck edge 10 (10, 12, 12) sts once, 8 (10, 10, 12) sts once.

Sleeves

With smaller needles, cast on 37 (41, 45, 49) sts. Work in k1, p1 rib for 1"/2.5cm, inc 9 (11, 11, 13) sts across last row—46 (52, 56, 62) sts. Change to larger needles.

BEGIN PATTERNS

Next row (RS) K1, work 11 (14, 16, 19) sts in moss st, 22 sts of cable panel, 11 (14, 16, 19) sts in moss st, k1.
Cont in pats as established, inc 1 st each side (working inc sts into moss st) every 4th row 4 (4, 5, 5) times, then every 8th row 3 (4, 4, 5) times—60 (68, 74, 82) sts. Work even until piece measures 6 (7, 8, 9)"/15 (17.5, 20, 22.5)cm from beg.

SHAPE CAP

Bind off 3 sts at beg of next 2 rows, 1 st at beg of next 4 rows. Bind off rem 50 (58, 64, 72) sts.

Finishing

Block pieces. Sew shoulder seams.

COLLAR

With RS facing and smaller needles, pick up and k 99 (102, 105, 107) sts around neck edge. Work in k1, p1 rib for ¾"/2cm. Bind off, do not break yarn. Place markers for buttons on left side of placket with top button at base of collar. With crochet hook, single crochet along sides of placket, making a chain-10 button loop opposite markers. Sew on buttons.

LEG BANDS

With RS facing and smaller needles, pick up and k 88 (104, 112, 120) sts across front leg opening, excluding rib. Work in k1, p1 rib for ½"/1.5cm. Bind off in rib. Rep for back leg opening. Cut 2 pieces snap tape plus 1"/2.5cm. Fold under ½"/1.5cm on each end of snap tape and sew to WS of leg bands. Fold leg bands to inside. Sew leg cuff seams. Sew side and underarm seams. ∎

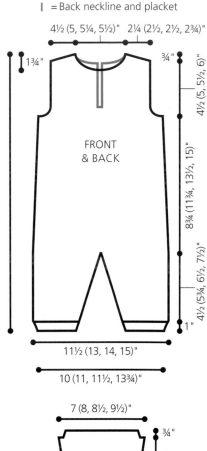

I = Back neckline and placket

4½ (5, 5¼, 5½)"   2¼ (2½, 2½, 2¾)"

1¾"

¾"

4½ (5, 5½, 6)"

FRONT & BACK

19¼ (24¼, 27¼, 30¼)"

8¾ (11¾, 13½, 15)"

4½ (5¾, 6½, 7½)"

1"

11½ (13, 14, 15)"

10 (11, 11½, 13¾)"

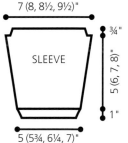

7 (8, 8½, 9½)"

¾"

SLEEVE

5 (6, 7, 8)"

1"

5 (5¾, 6¼, 7)"

Geometric Rattles

Babies love color, shape, and sound, and these soft and squishy
rattles combine all three for boundless delight.

DESIGNED BY RACHEL MAURER

Knitted Measurements
Diameter after stuffing Approx 6"/15cm

Materials
- 1 3½oz/100g skein (each approx 240yd/220m) of Cascade Yarns *Cherub Aran Sparkle* (nylon/acrylic/metallic) each in #202 yellow (A), #210 blue (B), and #204 green (C)
- 2 sets (5 each) size 4 (3.5mm) double-pointed needles (dpns) *or size to obtain gauge*
- Stitch markers
- Scrap yarn and crochet hook for provisional cast-on
- Fiberfill stuffing
- 3 empty small plastic bubble gum machine capsules
- Small buttons or beads for rattle
- Tape

Provisional Cast-On
With scrap yarn and crochet hook, chain the number of sts to cast on plus a few extra. Cut a tail and pull the tail through the last chain. With knitting needle and yarn, pick up and knit the stated number of sts through the "bumps" on the back of the chain. To remove scrap yarn chain, when instructed, pull out the tail from the last crochet stitch. Gently and slowly pull on the tail to unravel the crochet stitches, carefully placing each released knit stitch on a needle.

Gauge
21 sts and 28 rows to 4"/10cm over St st using size 4 (3.5mm) needles.
Take time to check gauge.

Geometric Rattles

Circle

With A, cast on 80 sts using provisional cast-on method. Knit 1 row. Join, being careful not to twist sts, and place marker (pm) for beg of rnd.

FIRST SIDE

Next (set-up) rnd [K10, pm] 7 times, k10.
Next (dec) rnd [K to 2 sts before marker, k2tog, sl marker] 8 times—8 sts dec'd.
Rep dec rnd every 3rd rnd 4 times more—40 sts.
Break yarn. Place sts on scrap yarn to hold.

SECOND SIDE

Carefully remove scrap yarn from provisional cast-on and place sts on dpns. Work as for first side. Break yarn, leaving tail approx 1yd/1m long for grafting.

Finishing

Fill plastic capsule with buttons or beads, being careful not to overfill. Tape securely shut. Wrap in small amount of fiberfill. Set aside. Weave in ends. Place held sts on 2nd set of dpns and fold piece in half so WS are tog. Graft sts tog using Kitchener st, stuffing as you go. Place capsule inside, being sure it is well padded on all sides.

Square

With B, cast on 96 sts using provisional cast-on method. Knit one row. Join, being careful not to twist sts, and pm for beg of rnd.

FIRST SIDE

Knit one rnd.
Rnd 1 (dec) K10, [S2KP, k21] 3 times, S2KP, k11—88 sts.
Rnds 2 and 3 Knit.
Rnd 4 (dec) K9, [S2KP, k19] 3 times, S2KP, k10—80 sts.
Rnds 5 and 6 Knit.
Rnd 7 (dec) K8, [S2KP, k17] 3 times, S2KP, k9—72 sts.
Rnds 8 and 9 Knit.
Rnd 10 (dec) K7, [S2KP, k15] 3 times, S2KP, k8—64 sts.
Rnds 11 and 12 Knit.
Rnd 13 (dec) K6, [S2KP, k13] 3 times, S2KP, k7—56 sts.
Rnds 14 and 15 Knit.
Rnd 16 (dec) K5, [S2KP, k11] 3 times, S2KP, k6—48 sts.
Rnds 17 and 18 Knit.
Break yarn. Place sts on scrap yarn to hold.

SECOND SIDE

Carefully remove scrap yarn from provisional cast-on and place sts on dpns.
Work as for first side. Break yarn, leaving tail approx 1yd/1m long for grafting.

Finishing

Finish as for circle.

Triangle

With C, cast on 72 sts using provisional cast-on method. Knit one row. Join, being careful not to twist sts, and pm for beg of rnd.

FIRST SIDE

Knit 1 rnd.
Rnd 1 (dec) K10, [S2KP, k21] twice, S2KP, k11—66 sts.
Rnds 2 and 3 Knit.
Rnd 4 (dec) K9, [S2KP, k19) twice, S2KP, k10—60 sts.
Rnds 5 and 6 Knit.
Rnd 7 (dec) K8, [S2KP, k17] twice, S2KP, k9—54 sts.
Rnds 8 and 9 Knit.
Rnd 10 (dec) K7, [S2KP, k15] twice, S2KP, k8—48 sts.
Rnds 11 and 12 Knit.
Rnd 13 (dec) K6, [S2KP, k13] twice, S2KP, k7—42 sts.
Rnds 14 and 15 Knit.
Rnd 16 (dec) K5, [S2KP, k11] twice, S2KP, k6—36 sts.
Rnds 17 and 18 Knit.
Break yarn. Place sts on scrap yarn to hold.

SECOND SIDE

Carefully remove scrap yarn from provisional cast-on and place sts on dpns. Work as for first side. Break yarn, leaving tail approx 1yd/1m long for grafting.

Finishing

Finish as for circle. ∎

Twisted Diamonds Afghan

This graphic, textural baby blanket features twisted stitches on a garter stitch background. Make it in any color to match the nursery!

DESIGNED BY MARGARET WILSON

Knitted Measurements
Approx 30 x 36"/77.5 x 91.5cm

Materials
■ 5 3½oz/100g skeins (each approx 240yd/220m) of Cascade Yarns *Cherub Aran Sparkle* (nylon/acrylic/metallic) in #205 coral

■ Size 7 (4.5mm) circular needle, 24"/60cm long, *or size to obtain gauge*

Stitch Glossary
2-st RT K2tog, without dropping sts from LH needle, k the first st again and let sts drop from LH needle.
2-st LT Skip first st on LH needle, k 2nd st tbl, k first and 2nd sts tog tbl.

Afghan
Cast on 170 sts.
Knit 6 rows.
Set-up row (WS) K5 for border, [p5, k10, p5] 8 times across, k to end.

BEGIN CHART
Row 1 (RS) K5, work 20-st rep 8 times across, k5.
Cont to work chart in this manner, keeping sts outside of chart pat in garter st (k every row), until row 20 is complete.
Rep rows 1–20 for 13 times more.
Knit 6 rows.
Bind off. ■

STITCH KEY

□	k on RS, p on WS	⊠ 2-st RT
−	p on RS, k on WS	⊠ 2-st LT

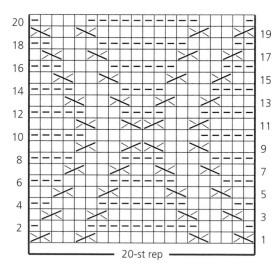

20-st rep

Gauge
22 sts and 33 rows to 4"/10cm over chart pat using size 7 (4.5mm) needle. *Take time to check gauge.*

24

Mini Mackintosh

Step out in the rain in style with a pint-size take on the classic trench, complete with toggle buttons and notched lapels.

DESIGNED BY CHRISTINA BEHNKE

Sizes
Instructions are written for size 6 months (12 months, 18 months). Shown in size 6 months.

Knitted Measurements
Chest (closed) 22 (24, 26)"/56 (61, 66)cm
Length 12 (13, 14)"/30.5 (33, 35.5)cm
Upper arm 6½ (7½, 8½)"/16.5 (19, 21.5)cm

Materials
■ 2 (2, 3) 3½oz/100g skeins (each approx 240yd/220m) of Cascade Yarns *Cherub Aran* (nylon/acrylic) in #43 golden rod

■ Size 6 (4mm) circular needle, 24"/60cm long, *or size to obtain gauge*

■ One set (5) size 6 (4mm) double-pointed needles (dpns)

■ Three ½"/12mm wooden toggle buttons

■ Stitch markers

■ Scrap yarn

✳ Pattern for Bow Beret is on page 190.

Stitch Glossary
M1R Insert LH needle from back to front under the strand between last st worked and next st on LH needle. K into the front loop to twist the st—1 st inc'd.
M1L Insert LH needle from front to back under the strand between last st worked and next st on LH needle. K into the back loop to twist the st—1 st inc'd.
kfb Knit into front and back of next st—1 st inc'd.

Notes
1) Yoke and body are worked back and forth in rows from the top down. Circular needle is used to accommodate large number of sts.
2) Sleeves are worked in the round.
3) Sleeves are designed to be worn cuffed.

Mackintosh
YOKE
With circular needle, cast on 75 sts.
Set-up row (WS) K20, place marker (pm), k3, pm, k29, pm, k3, pm, k to end.
Next (inc) row (RS) [K to 1 st before marker, kfb, sl marker, kfb] 4 times—8 sts inc'd.
Working in garter st (k every row), rep inc row every other row 16 (19, 22) times more—211 (235, 259) sts. Knit 1 row.

DIVIDE FOR BODY AND SLEEVES
Next row (RS) K to marker, remove marker, place next 37 (43, 49) sts on scrap yarn for sleeve, remove marker, k63 (69, 75) for back, remove marker, place next 37 (43, 49) sts on scrap yarn for sleeve, remove marker, k to end—137 (149, 161) sts.
Next row (WS) K11 for left front band, pm, p to last 11 sts, pm, k11 for right front band.

Gauge
23 sts and 40 rows to 4"/10cm over garter stitch using size 6 (4mm) needles. *Take time to check gauge.*

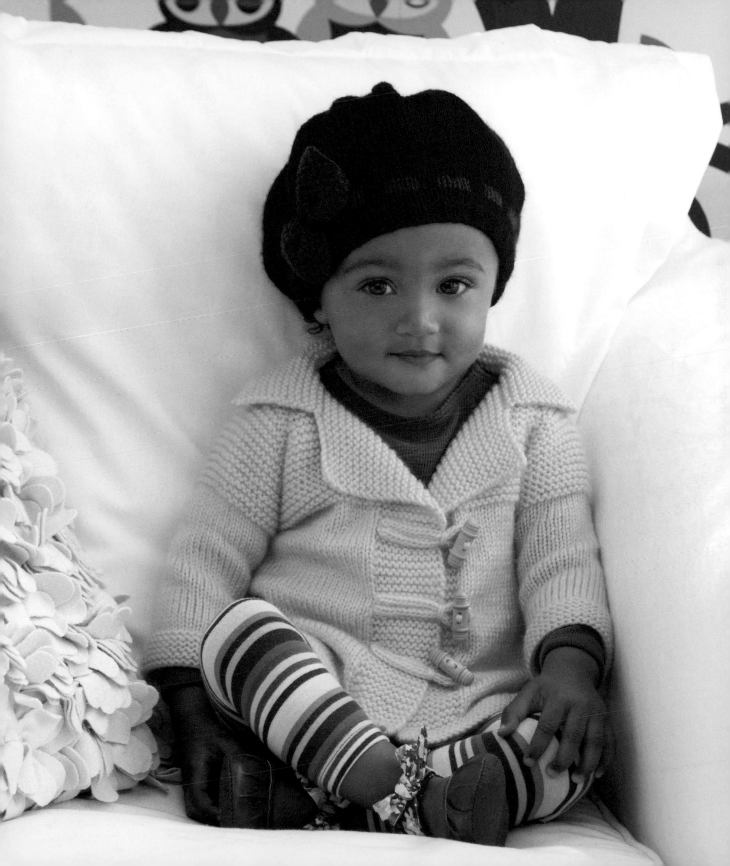

Mini Mackintosh

Working left and right front bands in garter st and body in St st (k on RS, p on WS), work even until piece measures 11 (12, 13)"/28 (30.5, 33)cm from back neck, end with a RS row.
Work 10 rows in garter st. Bind off.

SLEEVES
Place 37 (43, 49) sleeve sts from scrap on 4 dpns. Join and pm for beg of rnd. Work in St st (k every rnd) until sleeve measures 5 (6½, 7)"/12.5 (16.5, 18)cm from under arm. Work 10 rnds in garter st (k 1 rnd, p 1 rnd). Bind off purlwise.

Finishing
Lightly block garment to measurements.

COLLAR
Place markers for collar 11 sts in from each side along cast-on edge.
With WS facing and circular needle, beg at first collar marker, pick up and k 11 sts along left front neck edge, pm, pick up and k 32 sts evenly along back neck, pm, pick up and k 11 sts evenly to next marker—54 sts.
Rows 1 and 2 Knit.
Row 3 (inc) K to marker, M1L, sl marker,

k to next marker, sl marker, M1R, k to end—2 sts inc'd.
Row 4 Knit.
Rep rows 1–4 for 4 times more—64 sts. Knit 3 rows even. Bind off.

LEFT FRONT TOGGLES
Using a length of yarn, sew 3 toggles 2"/5cm in from edge of left front band, placing the first 3½"/9cm above lower edge, the top toggle 5 rows below last purl ridge of yoke, and the middle one centered in between.

I-CORD TOGGLE LOOPS
With dpn, cast on 3 sts. *Knit 1 row. Without turning work, slide sts to opposite end of needle to work the next row from the RS. Pull yarn tightly from end of row. Rep from * until I-cord measures 5½"/14cm. Break yarn, leaving a long tail, and draw tail through open sts to fasten off. Fold I-cord in half, leaving a loop just long enough for toggle to pass through. With length of yarn, wrap the cords tog several times. With ends of wrapping length, sew cord to right front band, securing ends at edge of band. Rep for each toggle. ■

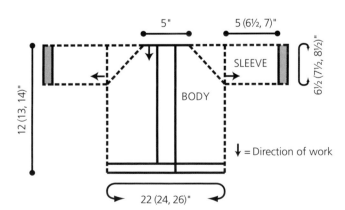

5" 5 (6½, 7)"

SLEEVE

6½ (7½, 8½)"

12 (13, 14)"

BODY

↓ = Direction of work

22 (24, 26)"

Lacy Cardi

Add some fanciful flower buttons to make this
delicate all-seasons cardigan even sweeter.

DESIGNED BY LORI STEINBERG

Sizes
Instructions are written for size
3 months (6 months, 12 months).
Shown in size 6 months.

Knitted Measurements
Chest (closed) 19 (20, 21)"/48
(51, 53.5)cm
Length 11¼ (12, 12¾)"/28.5
(30.5, 32.5)cm
Upper arm 9½ (10, 10½)"/24
(25.5, 26.5)cm

Materials
■ 2 (2, 3) 1¾oz/50g skeins (each approx
180yd/165m) of Cascade Yarns *Cherub
DK* (nylon/acrylic) in #45 raspberry

■ One pair size 6 (4mm) needles *or size
to obtain gauge*

■ Size 6 (4mm) circular needle, 24"/60cm
long, for edging

■ Size G/6 (4mm) crochet hook for
button loop

■ Five ⅞"/22mm buttons

■ Removable stitch markers

Stitch Glossary
kfbf Knit into the front, back, and front
of the next st to inc 2 sts.

Note
Garter stitch borders and edgings are
picked up and knit in finishing.

Cardigan
With straight needles, cast on 94 (103,
112) sts. Purl 1 row.

BEGIN CHART
Row 1 (RS) Work to rep line, work 9-st
rep 10 (11, 12) times across, work to end
of chart.

Cont to work chart in this way until row
18 is complete. Rep rows 1–18 until
piece measures 5½ (6, 6½)"/14 (15,
16.5)cm from beg, end with a WS row.

DIVIDE FOR FRONTS AND BACK
Next row (RS) Work 30 (33, 38) sts, bind
off 2 sts for armhole, cont in pat as
established until there are 45 (48, 50) sts
on needle after bind-off, bind off 2 sts
for 2nd armhole, work in pat to end.
Working 3 sections at once with separate
balls of yarn, cont in pat until armhole
measures 2¾ (3, 3¼)"/7 (7.5, 8)cm, end
with a WS row.

SHAPE NECK
Next row (RS) With first ball of yarn,
bind off 21 (23, 27) sts for right front
neck, work to end of row with separate
balls of yarn.
Next row (WS) With first ball of yarn,
bind off 6 (8, 9) sts for left front neck,
work to end of row with separate balls of
yarn—9 (10, 11) sts for each front
shoulder, 45 (48, 50) sts for back.
Cont in pat on rem sts until piece
measures 10¼ (11, 11¾)"/26 (28, 30)cm
from beg, end with a WS row. Bind off.

Gauge
19 sts and 32 rows to 4"/10cm over chart pat using size 6 (4mm) needles. *Take time to check gauge.*

Lacy Cardi

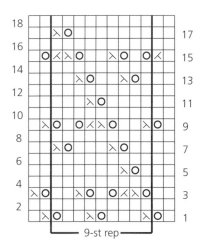

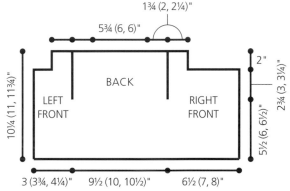

STITCH KEY

- ☐ k on RS, p on WS
- ☒ k2tog
- ☒ SKP
- ☐ yo

Sleeves

With straight needles, cast on 40 sts.
Purl 1 row.

BEGIN CHART

Next row (RS) Work to rep line, work 9-st rep 4 times across, work to end of chart. Cont to work chart in this way until row 18 is complete. Rep rows 1 and 2 once more.

SHAPE SLEEVE

Cont in chart pat as established and working inc'd sts into pat, inc 1 st each side of next row, then every 12th row 2 (3, 4) times more—46 (48, 50) sts. Work even as established until sleeve measures 8 (9, 10)"/20.5 (23, 25.5)cm from beg. Bind off.

Finishing

Sew shoulder seams. Sew sleeves into armholes. Sew sleeve seams. Place markers for 4 buttons on the left front, approx ½"/1.5cm from the edge, with center of first button just ½"/1.5cm from the neck edge, center of 4th button 3½"/9cm from the neck edge, and other 2 buttons evenly spaced between.

BUTTONHOLE BAND

With RS facing and straight needle, pick up and k 50 (54, 58) sts along right front edge. Work in garter st (k every row) for 9 rows.
Next (buttonhole) row (RS) Cont in garter st, working buttonholes to correspond to markers as foll: yo, k2tog. Work 4 rows more in garter st. Bind off.

EDGING

With circular needle, beg at top of buttonhole band, with RS facing, pick up and k 6 sts along top of buttonhole band, pick up and k 21 (23, 27) sts along right front neck, pick up and k 2 sts along side edge of right neck and place marker (pm) in 2nd st, pick up and k 10 sts more, pm in last st, pick up and k 27 (28, 28) sts along back neck, pick up and

k 12 sts along left neck, placing marker in first and last of these sts; pick up and k 5 (7, 8) sts along left front neck, pick up and k 2 sts in next st along left front neck, pm in 2nd of these sts; pick up and k 50 (54, 58) sts along left front edge— 135 (144, 153) sts.
Knit 1 row, moving markers up.
Next row (RS) [K to 1 st before next marker, S2KP, move marker up] 4 times, k to next marker, kfbf in marked st, k to end.
Rep last 2 rows 3 times more. Knit 1 row. Bind off.

LOWER BORDER

With circular needle, pick up and k 94 (103, 112) sts along cast-on edge. Knit 4 rows. Bind off.

BUTTON LOOP

With crochet hook, beg at side edge of neckband above buttonhole band, work 3 sc in side of neck band, ch 4 for button loop, sc in last row of neckband. Fasten off.
Sew button to correspond to loop, sew 4 buttons as marked. ■

26
Mouse-mobile

Ready, set, go! Cute and cool details make this toy a treat, from the mouse's racing helmet and scarf to the car's grille and bright hubcaps.

DESIGNED BY MEGAN KREINER

Knitted Measurements
Height of mouse Approx 5"/12.5cm
Length of car Approx 6"/15cm

Materials
- 1 3½oz/100g skein (each approx 240yd/220m) of Cascade Yarns *Cherub Aran* (nylon/acrylic) each in #17 grey (A), #35 taupe (B), #40 black (C), #01 white (D), #25 ruby (E), and #43 goldenrod (F)
- One set (5) size 5 (3.75mm) double-pointed needles (dpns) *or size to obtain gauge*
- One pair size 5 (3.75mm) needles
- Stitch markers
- Straight pins, embroidery needle
- Small amount of pink felt, matching thread and sewing needle

Short Row Wrap and Turn (w&t)
on RS row (on WS row)
1) Wyib (wyif), sl next st purlwise.
2) Move yarn between the needles to the front (back).
3) Sl the same st back to LH needle. Turn work. One st is wrapped.

4) When working the wrapped st, insert RH needle under the wrap and work it tog with the corresponding st on needle to hide or close wrap.

Note
Weave in ends as you work.

Mouse Body
With A and dpns, cast on 10 sts. Join, being careful not to twist sts, and place marker (pm) for beg of rnd.
Set-up rnd [Kfb, pm] 9 times, kfb—20 sts.

Next rnd Knit, slipping markers.
Next (inc) rnd [K to 1 st before marker, M1, k1, sl marker] 10 times around—10 sts inc'd.
Cont in St st and rep inc rnd every 4th rnd once more—40 sts.
Knit 3 rnds.
Next (dec) rnd [K to 2 sts before marker, k2tog, sl marker] 10 times around—10 sts dec'd.
Rep dec rnd every 4th rnd once more—20 sts.
Knit 3 rnds.
Next (dec) rnd [K3, k2tog] 4 times around—16 sts. Knit 3 rnds. Stuff body. Bind off. Break yarn.

Head
With A and dpns, cast on 6 sts. Join, being careful not to twist sts, and pm for beg of rnd.
Rnd 1 Kfb in each st around—12 sts.
Rnd 2 Knit.
Next (inc) rnd [K1, M1, k1] 6 times around—18 sts.
Knit 3 rnds.
Next (dec) rnd [K1, k2tog] 6 times around—12 sts.
Knit 3 rnds. Stuff head.

Gauge
24 sts and 32 rnds to 4"/10cm over St st using size 5 (3.75mm) needles. *Take time to check gauge.*

Mouse-mobile

SHAPE NOSE
Next (dec) rnd [K2tog] 6 times around—6 sts.
Knit 3 rnds.
Break A and thread tail through open sts. Pull tightly to close.

EARS (MAKE 2)
With A, cast on 4 sts. Do not join.
Next (inc) row Kfb in each st across—8 sts.
Next row P8.
Short rows (RS) K8, w&t; p4, w&t; k3, w&t; p2, w&t; k1, w&t; p to end of row.
Next row (RS) Knit.
Dec 1 st each side on next 2 rows—4 sts.
Break A, and thread tail through 4 open sts. Pull tightly to close.

PAWS (MAKE 4)
With B, cast on 4 sts. Join, being careful not to twist sts, and pm for beg of rnd.
Next (inc) rnd Kfb in each st around—8 sts.
Knit 3 rnds.
Next (dec) rnd [K2tog] 4 times around—4 sts.
Break B and thread tail through open sts. Pull tightly to close.

Racing Helmet
With D and dpns, cast on 6 sts. Join, being careful not to twist sts, and pm for beg of rnd.
Set-up rnd [Kfb, pm] 5 times, kfb—12 sts.
Next rnd Knit.
Next (inc) rnd [K to 1 st before marker, M1, k1, sl marker] 6 times around—6 sts inc'd.
Cont in St st and rep inc rnd every other rnd 4 times more—42 sts.
Knit 3 rnds.
Next (dec) rnd [K to 2 sts before

marker, k2tog, sl marker] 6 times around—6 sts dec'd.
Rep dec rnd once more—30 sts.
Next (ear hole) rnd [K3, k2tog, (yo) twice, ssk, k1, k2tog, (yo) twice, ssk, k3] twice.
Next rnd Knit, working k1, p1 in each double yo.
Next (dec) rnd [K to 2 sts before marker, k2tog, sl marker] 6 times around—6 sts dec'd.
Rep dec rnd *every* rnd 3 times more—6 sts.
Break D and thread tail through open sts. Pull tightly to close.

Helmet Stripe
With E and dpn, cast on 6 sts. *K6, do not turn, but slide sts to opposite end of needle to work next row from RS; rep from * for I-cord until 22 rows have been worked. Bind off.

Scarf
With D and dpn, cast on 6 sts. *K6, do not turn, but slide sts to opposite end of needle to work next row from RS; rep from * for I-cord until 40 rows have been worked. Bind off.

Finishing the Mouse
Using photo as guide, embroider eyes, nose, and eyebrows on face with C, using French knots for the eyes and nose and straight stitches for the eyebrows. Cut circles out of pink felt and sew to center of ears. Sew ears to sides of head. With A, whipstitch head to the open edge of the body. With B, make a tail out of twisted cord and sew in place. Flatten the helmet and fold, matching the ear holes. Place the helmet on the mouse's head and slip the ears through the holes. Pin the edge of the helmet

in place around the mouse's head. Pin to shape and sew in place. Flatten the racing stripe and sew to the top of the helmet.
Place the scarf around the mouse's neck and fasten in place by wrapping a length of yarn around the scarf ends close to the mouse's neck.
Cut six 3"/7.5cm strands of E and add to ends of scarf for fringe. Trim.

Car
RIGHT SIDE
Note Wind off a small ball of E to work the intarsia racing medallion. With E and straight needles, cast on 34 sts.
Next (inc) row (RS) K1, M1, k to end—35 sts.
Purl 1 row.

BEG MEDALLION
Row 1 (inc RS) K1, M1, k17, join D, k2, join a 2nd small ball of E, k15—36 sts.
Row 2 P14 E, p4 D, p18 E.
Row 3 K17 E, k6 D, k13 E.
Row 4 P12 E, p8 D, p16 E.
Row 5 K16 E, k8 D, k12 E.
Row 6 P12 E, k8, p16 E.
Row 7 Rep row 3.
Row 8 Rep row 2.
Row 9 (dec) K18 E, k2 D, k13 E, k2tog—35 sts. Break D.
Row 10 (dec) P2tog, p to end—34 sts.

DIVIDE TO SHAPE FRONT OF SIDE
Next row (RS) K2tog, k7.
Working on these 8 sts only, turn and cont shaping for front of car as foll:
Next row P to last 2 sts, p2tog.
Next row K2tog, k to end.
Next row P to last 2 sts, p2tog.
Next row K2tog, k1, k2tog.
Bind off rem 3 sts.

SHAPE CENTER OF SIDE

Rejoin yarn to center 10 sts for center tab. Pm in each end of this row for finishing.

Work 15 rows in St st. Pm in each end of this row for finishing. Bind off.

SHAPE BACK OF SIDE

Rejoin yarn to rem sts.

Next row (RS) K to last 2 sts, k2tog.
Next row P to last 2 sts, p2tog.
Next row K2tog, k to end.
Bind off rem 12 sts.

Left Side

Work as for right side, reversing all shaping.

Center of Car

Note This piece is one shaped strip that begins at the back opening and goes to the top of the back, then the bottom of the car is worked and then the hood and front opening.

With E and straight needles, cast on 12 sts. Pm in each end of first row for finishing.

Work in St st for 14 rows.

Cont in St st, dec 1 st each side every row 3 times—6 sts.

Break E.

With D, work 21 rows even, end with a WS row. Break D. Pm in each end of this row for finishing.

With C, cont in St st and inc 1 st each side every row 3 times—12 sts.

Work 21 rows even, end with a WS row. Break C.

With E, work 3 rows even.

BEG GRILLE

Row 1 (WS) P5 E, p2 A, p5 E.
Row 2 K5 E, k2 A, k5 E.
Row 3 P4 E, p4 A, p4 E.

Row 4 K4 E, k4 A, k4 E.
Row 5 P3 E, p6 A, p3 E.
Row 6 K3 E, k6 A, k3 E.
Row 7 P2 E, p8 A, p2 E.
Row 8 K2 E, k8 A, k2 E.
Row 9 P2 E, p8 A, p2 E.
Next (dec) row (RS) K2tog E, k1 E, k6 A, k1 E, k2tog E—10 sts.
Next (dec) row (WS) P2tog E, p1 E, p4 A, p1 E, p2tog E—8 sts. Break E and A.
Next (dec) row (RS) With D, k2tog, k4, k2tog—6 sts.
Work 12 rows even. Break D. Pm in each end of this row for finishing.
With E, inc 1 st each side 3 times—12 sts.

Work 10 rows even. Pm in each end of last row for finishing.
Bind off.

Back Tires (make 2)

With C and dpns, cast on 6 sts. Join, being careful not to twist sts, and pm for beg of rnd.
Set-up rnd [Kfb, pm] 5 times, kfb—12 sts.
Next rnd Knit, slipping markers.
Next (inc) rnd [K to 1 st before marker, M1, k1, sl marker] 6 times around—6 sts inc'd.
Cont in St st and rep inc rnd every other rnd 3 times more—36 sts.
Work 3 rnds even.

Hubcap (make 4)

With F and dpns, cast on 6 sts.
Join, being careful not to twist sts, and pm for beg of rnd.
Next rnd [Kfb] 6 times.
Work 3 rnds even in St st.
Next rnd [K2tog] 6 times.
Break F and thread tail through open sts.
Pull tightly to close.

Finishing the Car

With E, embroider a chain around each of the racing medallions. With A, embroider a chain around the grille. With C, embroider a number inside the medallions and straight stitches inside the grill, using photo as guide.

ASSEMBLY

Line up the 3 car pieces (right, left, and center) so they are facing the same direction with the center piece between the right and left sides. Sew the right and left fronts to each side of the front center section, beg with the first row of E and ending at the first set of markers. Sew the right and left backs to each side of the back center section, beg with the first row of D and ending at the first set of markers. Fold the side center tabs down so the last marked rows match the last marked row of the center piece at the front and back of the car. Sew these 4 seams between the markers to form the inside of the car. Stuff the front and back sections of the car, leaving the middle unstuffed. Push the inside of the car to the inside and sew the edge to the bottom of the car. Sew the hubcaps to the center of the tires and sew the tires to the car, using photo as guide.
Place the mouse in the car. ∎

Next (dec) rnd [K to 2 sts before marker, k2tog] 6 times around—6 sts dec'd.
Rep dec rnd every other rnd 3 times more—12 sts.
Work 1 rnd even.
Stuff wheel.
Next (dec) rnd [K2tog] 6 times around—6 sts. Break C and thread tail through open sts. Thread the tail through the center of the tire 4 times, pulling tightly to shape the tire.

Front Tires (make 2)

With C and dpns, cast on 6 sts. Join, being careful not to twist sts, and pm for beg of rnd.

Set-up rnd [Kfb, pm] 5 times, kfb—12 sts.
Next rnd Knit, slipping markers.
Next (inc) rnd [K to 1 st before marker, M1, k1, sl marker] 6 times around—6 sts inc'd.
Cont in St st and rep inc rnd every other rnd once more—24 sts.
Work 3 rnds even.
Next (dec) rnd [K to 2 sts before marker, k2tog] 6 times around—6 sts dec'd.
Rep dec rnd every other rnd once more—12 sts.
Complete as for back tire.

Kitty-Cat Pullover

The details that make this sweater unique are small but special: an embroidered kitty face, a dainty bow, and delicate buttons.

DESIGNED BY PAT OLSKI

Sizes

Instructions are written for size 6 months (12 months, 18 months). Shown in size 6 months.

Knitted Measurements

Chest 20 (21, 22)"/51 (53, 56)cm
Length 11½ (12¾, 13)"/29 (31, 33)cm
Upper arm 8 (8½, 8¾)"/20.5 (21.5, 22)cm

Materials

■ 1 (2, 2) 1¾oz/50g skeins (each approx 180yd/165m) of Cascade Yarns *Cherub DK* (nylon/acrylic) in #53 mauve orchid (A) and #7 baby lavender (B)

■ 1 skein in #40 black (C)

■ One each sizes 3 and 5 (3.25 and 3.75mm) circular needle, 24"/60cm long, *or size to obtain gauge*

■ Stitch markers, stitch holders

■ Three ½"/12mm buttons

■ Embroidery (or tapestry) needle

K1, P1 Rib

(over an even number of sts)
Row/rnd 1 (RS) *K1, p1; rep from * around.
Rep row/rnd 1 for k1, p1 rib.

3-Needle Bind-Off

1) Hold right sides of pieces together on 2 needles. Insert 3rd needle knitwise into first st of each needle, and wrap yarn knitwise.
2) Knit these 2 sts together, and slip them off the needles. *Knit the next 2 sts together in the same manner.
3) Slip first st on 3rd needle over 2nd st and off needle. Rep from * in step 2 across row until all sts are bound off.

Pullover Body

With smaller needles and A, cast on 114 (120, 126) sts. Join, being careful not to twist sts, and place marker (pm) for beg of rnds. Work in k1, p1 rib for 1"/2.5cm.

Change to larger needles and B. Work in St st (k every rnd) until piece measures 7½ (8, 8½)"/19 (20.5, 21.5)cm from beg.

DIVIDE FOR FRONT AND BACK

Row 1 Bind off 3 sts, k until there are 51 (54, 57) sts, leave these on hold for front, bind off 6 sts, k until there are 51 (54, 57) sts on needle, join new end of yarn, bind off rem 3 sts. Turn and, working back and forth in rows on back sts only, work as foll:
Next row (WS) Purl.
Dec row (RS) K2, k2tog, k to last 4 sts, ssk, k2—2 sts dec'd.
Rep last 2 rows 3 times more—43 (46, 49) sts. Work even until armhole measures 3½ (3¾, 4)"/9 (9.5, 10)cm.

SHAPE NECK

Row 1 (RS) K12 (13, 14), with 2nd skein bind off 19 (20, 21) sts, k to end.
Row 2 Working both sides at once with separate skeins, purl sts on each side of neck.
Row 3 First side, k8 (9, 10), k2tog, k2; 2nd side, K2, ssk, k to end. Sl rem 11 (12, 13) sts each side to st holders.

Gauge

23 sts and 30 rows to 4"/10cm over St st using size 5 (3.75mm) circular needle. *Take time to check gauge.*

27
Kitty-Cat Pullover

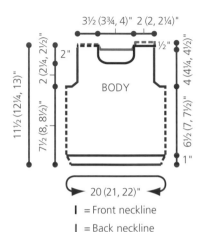

3½ (3¾, 4)" 2 (2, 2¼)"

½"

2"

BODY

11½ (12¼, 13)"

2 (2¼, 2½)"

7½ (8, 8½)"

4 (4¼, 4½)"

6½ (7, 7½)"

1"

20 (21, 22)"

Ⅰ = Front neckline

Ⅰ = Back neckline

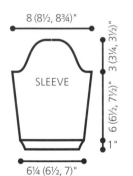

8 (8½, 8¾)"

SLEEVE

3 (3¼, 3½)"

6 (6½, 7½)"

1"

6¼ (6½, 7)"

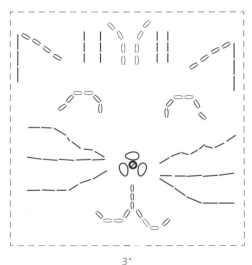

3"

3"

FRONT
Work same as back until armhole measures 2 (2¼, 2¾)"/5 (6, 6.5)cm.

SHAPE NECK
Row 1 (RS) K15 (16, 17), with 2nd skein bind off 13 (14, 15) sts, k to end.
Row 2 Working both sides at once with separate skeins, purl sts on each side.
Row 3 1st side: k to last 4 sts, k2tog, k2; 2nd side: k2, ssk, k to end—2 sts dec'd. Rep last 2 rows twice more—12 (13, 14) sts each side. Work sides as foll:

RIGHT SHOULDER
Next row (WS) Purl.
Next row (RS) K2, ssk, k to end—11 (12, 13) sts.
Work even until armhole measures 4 (4¼, 4½)"/10 (10.5, 11.5)cm. Using 3-needle bind-off worked from WS, join these sts tog with right back shoulder.

LEFT SHOULDER
Row 1 (RS) [K1, p1] 5 (5, 6) times, k2tog, k0 (1, 0)—11 (12, 13) sts.
Row 2 Work even in established rib.
Buttonhole row 3 Rib 4, yo, ssk, rib to end.
Rows 4 and 5 Work even in rib. Bind off. Work sts on hold for left back shoulder in rib for 6 rows, bind off.

STITCH KEY
3"

⊟ split stitch—2 ply

⊟ split stitch—2 ply

⊘ chain st—all ply

⦸ french knot—all ply

Sleeves
With smaller needles and C, cast on 36 (38, 40) sts. Work in k1, p1 rib for 1"/2.5cm. Change to larger needles and A. Work in St st, inc 1 st each side of every 4th row 5 times—46 (48, 50) sts. Work even until piece measures 7 (7½, 8½)"/18 (19, 21.5)cm from beg.

SHAPE CAP
Bind off 3 sts at beg of next 2 rows.
Dec row (RS) K2, k2tog, k to last 4 sts, ssk, k2—2 sts dec'd.
Rep dec row every other row 4 (5, 6) times, then every 4th row twice. Bind off 3 sts at beg of next 4 rows. Bind off rem 14 sts.

Finishing
Set in right sleeve. Set in left sleeve, eliminating back ribbed shoulder extension. Sew sleeve seams.

NECKBAND
With smaller needles and A, from the RS, pick up and k 64 (66, 68) sts around neck edge, ending just before shoulder extension. Work in k1, p1 rib for 1 row.
Buttonhole row (RS) Rib 4, yo, ssk, rib to end. Work 4 more rows in rib. Bind off in rib. Sew on buttons.

CAT
With C and tapestry needle, embroider cat face on lower left front, foll chart.

Bow
With smaller needle and B, cast on 14 sts.
Row 1 K to last st, sl last st wyib.
Row 2 P to last st, p last st wyif. Rep these 2 rows until piece measures 1½"/4cm. Bind off. With a long strand, wind yarn around center of piece and fasten to form a bow. With same strand, fasten to right neck edge, using photo as guide. ∎

28

Seeing Stars Blanket

Stripes and geometric shapes radiate to form a star in a creative construction worked out from the center medallion.

DESIGNED BY IRINA POLUDNENKO

■■■■

Knitted Measurements
Approx 30 x 30"/76 x 76cm
measured across center.

Materials

■ 2 3½oz/100g skeins (each approx 240yd/220m) of Cascade Yarns *Cherub Aran* (nylon/acrylic) each in #11 key lime (B) and #6 baby peach (D)

■ 1 skein each in #38 yellow (A) and #5 baby mint (C)

■ One set (5) size 6 (4mm) double-pointed needles (dpns) *or size to obtain gauge*

■ Two size 6 (4mm) circular needles, 16 and 24"/40 and 60cm long

■ 2 spare size 6 (4mm) circular needles, each 16"/40cm long

■ Safety pin

■ Stitch markers

■ Stitch holders

Stripe Pattern 1

Work in garter st 4 rnds A, 4 rnds B.
Rep these 8 rnds for stripe pat 1.

Stripe Pattern 2

Work in garter st 4 rnds A, 4 rnds C.
Rep these 8 rnds for stripe pat 2.

Stripe Pattern 3

Work in garter st 4 rnds D, 4 rnds B.
Rep these 8 rnds for stripe pat 3.

Blanket

With dpns and A, cast on 4 sts.
Join, being careful not to twist sts, and place marker (pm) for beg of rnd. Divide sts evenly on 4 dpns.

BEGIN STRIPE PAT 1

Rnd 1 *(K1, yo, k1) in same st; rep from * 3 times more—3 sts on each needle, 12 sts in rnd.
Rnd 2 Purl.
Rnd 3 [K1, (k1, yo, k1) in next st, k1] 4 times around—5 sts on each needle.
Rnd 4 Purl.
Rnd 5 With B, [Kfb, k to last st, kfb] 4 times—2 sts inc'd on each needle.
Rnd 6 Purl.
Cont in garter st (k 1 rnd, p 1 rnd) and stripe pat 1 as established, rep rnds 5 and

6 for 8 times more, then row 5 once—25 sts on each needle.
Next rnd With shorter circular needle, [p25, pm] 4 times around.
Next (inc) rnd [Kfb, k to 1 st before marker, kfb, sl marker] 4 times around—2 sts inc'd between each set of markers.
Purl 1 rnd.
Change to longer circular needle as needed.
Cont in stripe pat as established, rep inc rnd every other rnd 11 times more—49 sts between markers.
Purl 1 rnd. Break A and B.

BEGIN 2ND SECTION

[Place 49 sts on st holder] 3 times.
Working on last 49 sts only, beg stripe pat 2.
**Row 1 Place next 24 sts on spare needle, join A to next st, (k1, yo, k1) in this st, place next 24 sts on spare needle.
Row 2 (WS) With A, k3. Place marker in center st and move this marker up every row.
Row 3 (RS) Sl 1 knitwise, k to center st, (k1, yo, k1) in center st, k to last st, p last st tog with next st on spare needle.

Gauge

20 sts and 40 rows/rnds to 4"/10cm over garter st using size 6 (4mm) needles.
Take time to check gauge..

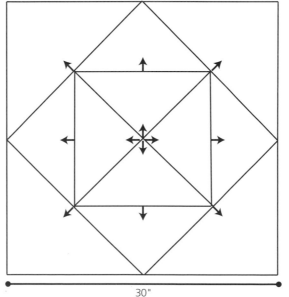

Seeing Stars Blanket

Row 4 (WS) Sl 1 knitwise, kfb, k to last 2 sts, kfb, k last st tog with next st on spare needle.

Cont in stripe pat 2 as established, rep rows 3 and 4 until all sts from spare needles have been worked—99 sts. Place 49 sts on st holder, place center st on safety pin, place last 49 sts on same st holder. Rep from ** for rem 3 sides.

BEGIN 3RD SECTION

***Place last 49 sts from one st holder on spare needle, place first 49 sts from next st holder on spare needle.

Row 1 With D, pick up and k 1 st between the 2 spare needles,
(k1, yo, k1) in this st, place next 24 sts on spare needle.

Row 2 (WS) K3. Place marker in center st and move this marker up every row.

Row 3 (RS) Sl 1 knitwise, k to center st, (k1, yo, k1) in center st, k to last st, p last st tog with next st on spare needle.

Row 4 (WS) Sl 1 knitwise, kfb, k to last 2 sts, kfb, k last st tog with next st on spare needle.

Cont in stripe pat 3 as established, rep rows 3 and 4 until all sts from spare needles have been worked—199 sts. Break D and B. Place sts on st holder. Rep from *** 3 times more.

Finishing

Join B and bind off all sts. ∎

↑ = Direction of work

30"

Funky Fair Isle Hat

The earflaps, colorwork, and tassel atop this cozy cap evoke the special style of a South American chullo.

DESIGNED BY LORNA MISER

Size
Instructions are written for size 6–24 months.

Knitted Measurements
Head circumference 16"/40.5cm
Length 6"/15cm

Materials
■ 1 3½oz/100g skein (each approx 240yd/220m) of Cascade Yarns *Cherub Aran* (nylon/acrylic) each in #48 methyl blue (A), #17 grey (B), and #21 grass (C)

■ One set (5) size 5 (3.75mm) double-pointed needles (dpns) *or size to obtain gauge*

■ Stitch marker

Hat
With A, cast on 80 sts. Join, being careful not to twist sts, and place marker for beg of rnd.
Beg with a purl rnd, work 5 rnds in garter st.
Next (inc) rnd [K10, M1] 8 times around—88 sts.

BEGIN LARGE CHECK PAT
Next 2 rnds *K2 A, k2 B; rep from * around.
Next 2 rnds *K2 B, k2 A; rep from * around.
Knit 1 rnd B, purl 1 rnd C, [knit 1 rnd B, knit 1 rnd C] 3 times, purl 1 rnd B.

Gauge
22 sts and 28 rnds to 4"/10cm over St st using size 5 (3.75mm) needles.
Take time to check gauge.

Funky Fair Isle Hat

Rnd 11 [K4 C, k2tog B] 8 times around—40 sts.
Rnd 12 [K4 C, k1 B] 8 times around.
Rnd 13 [K3 C, k2tog B] 8 times around—32 sts.
Rnd 14 [K3 C, k1 B] 8 times around.
Rnd 15 [K2 C, k2tog B] 8 times around—24 sts.
Rnd 16 [K2 C, k1 B] 8 times around.
Rnd 17 [K1 C, k2tog B] 8 times around—16 sts.
Rnd 18 [K1 C, k1 B] 8 times around.
Break yarn, leaving a long tail.
Thread 1 tail through rem sts to close.

Finishing

Make a 5"/14cm tassel using
all 3 colors and attach to top of hat.

EARFLAP
With beg of rnd as back of hat, count 10
sts from back of hat. With C, pick up and
k 12 sts along lower edge, working away
from back of hat. Knit 8 rows. Break C.
Next (dec) row With B, k1, k2tog,
k to last 3 sts, SKP, k1—2 sts dec'd.
Rep dec row every other row twice
more—6 sts. Knit 1 row. Bind off. Rep for
2nd earflap. ■

BEGIN LITTLE CHECK PAT
Rnd 1 *K1 A, k1 C; rep from * around.
Rnd 2 K1 B, k1 A; rep from * around.
Rep rnds 1 and 2 twice more.
Knit 1 rnd C, purl 1 rnd B, knit 1 rnd C.

Shape Crown

Rnd 1 With C, [k9, k2tog] 8 times around—80 sts.
Rnd 2 With A, knit.
Rnd 3 [K8 A, k2tog B] 8 times around—72 sts.
Rnd 4 [K8 A, k1 B] 8 times around.
Rnd 5 [K7 A, k2tog B] 8 times around—64 sts.
Rnd 6 [K7 A, k1 B] 8 times around.
Rnd 7 [K6 A, k2tog B] 8 times around—56 sts.
Rnd 8 [K6 C, k1 B] 8 times around.
Rnd 9 [K5 C, k2tog B] 8 times around—48 sts.
Rnd 10 [K5 C, k1 B] 8 times around.

 Pattern for Fancy Flared Jacket is on page 120.

30
Dotty Bunting
Abstract concentric circles add a sense of whimsical fun to a quirky, modern buttoned bunting.

DESIGNED BY GALINA CARROLL

Sizes
Instructions are written for size 3 months (6 months). Shown in size 6 months.

Knitted Measurements
Chest 18 (20)"/46 (51)cm
Length 18¼ (19)"/46.5 (48)cm

Materials
■ 1 1¾oz/50g skein (each approx 180yd/165m) of Cascade Yarns *Cherub DK* (nylon/acrylic) each in #09 ecru (A), #06 baby peach (B), #14 melon (C), #19 geranium (D), and #35 taupe (E)

■ One pair size 5 (3.75mm) needles *or size to obtain gauge*

■ One set (5) size 5 (3.75mm) double-pointed needles (dpns)

■ Four ½"/12.5mm buttons

■ Tapestry needle

■ Stitch markers, stitch holders

Notes
1) Bunting is worked flat in one piece.
2) Dots are worked using the intarsia method. Twist strands on WS when changing colors to avoid holes in work.
3) Use a separate bobbin or strand for each color section. Do not carry colors across WS of work.

K1, P1 Rib
(over an even number of sts)
Rnd 1 *K1, p1; rep from * to end.
Rep rnd 1 for k1, p1 rib.

Bunting
With A and larger needle, cast on 45 (50) front sts, place marker (pm) for side, cast on 45 (50) back sts—90 (100) sts total. Work in St st (k on RS, p on WS) for 8 rows.

BEG CHART 1
Next row (RS) With A, k18 (23), pm, work row 1 of chart 1 over next 27 sts, pm, with A, k to end.
Next row (WS) With A, p to first marker, sl marker, work row 2 of chart 1 to next marker, sl marker, with A, p to end.
Cont to work chart in this manner until row 29 of chart 1 is complete. Remove chart markers only. Cont in St st, with A, work 3 (6) rows, end with a WS row.

BEG CHART 2
Next row (RS) Work row 1 of chart 2 over next 14 sts, pm, with A, work to end.
Next row (WS) P to marker, sl marker, work row 2 of chart to end.
Cont in this manner until row 20 of chart 2 is complete. Remove chart marker only.
Next row (RS) With A, k19 (22), pm, k15, pm, k11 (13), work to end.
Cont in St st, slipping markers, until piece measures 11½ (12)"/29 (30.5)cm from beg, end with a WS row.

BODICE
Next row (RS) *K2, p2; rep from *, end k2 (0).
Next row K the knit sts and p the purl sts.
Rep the last 2 rows for k2, p2 rib for 1"/2.5cm, end with a WS row.
Work in St st for 4 rows.

SHAPE ARMHOLES
Next row (RS) Bind off 3 (4) sts for left armhole, work to 3 (4) sts before side marker, join 2nd ball of A, remove side marker, bind off 6 (8) sts for right armhole, work to end.
Next row (WS) Working both sides at once with separate balls of yarn, bind off 3 (4) sts for left armhole, p to end—39 (42) sts rem for each side.

Gauge
20 sts and 24 rows to 4"/10cm over St st using size 5 (3.75mm) needles. *Take time to check gauge.*

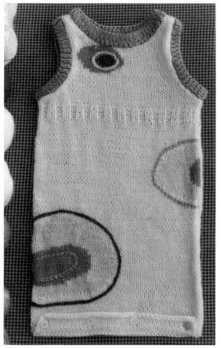

4½, (5¼)" 1"

FRONT
& BACK

5¼ (5½)"

1½"

18¼ (19)"

11½ (12)"

½"

18 (20)"

↑ = Direction of work

❙ = Back neckline and buttonhole flap

BEG CHART 3
Working on front sts only, dec 1 st at each armhole edge every RS row 3 times—33 (36) sts, AT THE SAME TIME, when 4 (6) rows have been worked, beg chart 3.
Next row (RS) With A, k to marker, sl marker, work row 1 of chart to next marker, sl marker, with A, work to end.
Next row With A, work to marker, sl marker, work chart row 2 to next marker, sl marker, with A, work to end.
Cont to work chart in this manner until row 12 of chart 3 is complete. Remove chart markers. With A, work 2 rows more.

SHAPE FRONT NECK
Next row (RS) Work 10 front sts, join a 2nd ball of A and bind off 13 (16) sts for neck, work to end—10 sts each side.
Next row (WS) Working both sides at once with separate balls of yarn, purl.
Cont to work both sides of front at once and dec 1 st at each neck edge every RS row 5 times—5 sts rem for each shoulder.
Work even until armhole measures 5¼ (5½)"/13.5 (14)cm, end with a WS row. Place shoulder sts on st holders.

BACK
Work armhole decs as for front, then work even until armhole measures 3¾ (4)"/9.5 (10)cm, end with a WS row.

SHAPE BACK NECK
Next row (RS) K7, join a 2nd ball of A and bind off 19 (22) sts, k to end—7 sts rem each side for shoulders.
Working both sides at once with separate balls of yarn, dec 1 st at back neck edges every RS row 2 times—5 sts rem each side.

Work even until same length as front, end with a RS row, leave sts on needle.

Finishing
Graft shoulder sts.
Using photo as guide for yarn color and placement, embroider chain st accents on each dot motif.
Sew side seam.

ARMHOLE AND NECK TRIM
With RS facing, dpns, and E, beg at underarm and pick up and k 78 (82) sts around armhole. Pm, join to work in rnd. Work 4 rnds of k1, p1 rib. Bind off. Rep for other armhole.
With RS facing, dpns and E, beg at left shoulder and pick up and k 94 (98) sts around neck edge. Pm, join to work in rnd. Work 5 rnds of k1, p1 rib. Bind off.

BUTTONHOLE FLAP
With RS facing, larger needle, and A, work along cast-on edge of back only and pick up and k 50 sts. Knit 1 row, purl 1 row, knit 1 row.
Next row (RS) Knit. Work in St st for 3 rows more.
Next (buttonhole) row (RS) K4, [yo, k2tog, k12] 3 times, yo, k2tog, k2.
Work in St st for 3 rows more. Bind off purlwise. Fold flap along purl ridge. Sew buttons to lower edge of front, opposite buttonholes. ■

CHART 1

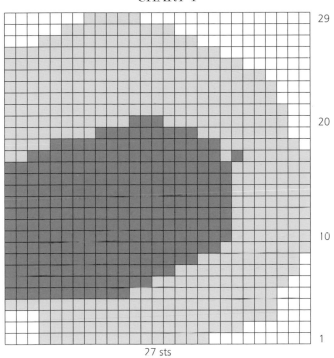

29

20

10

1

27 sts

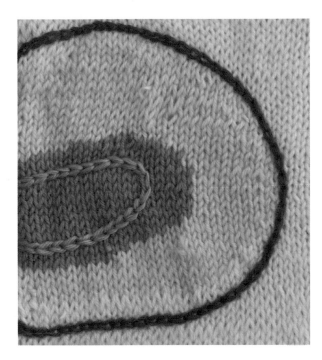

CHART 2

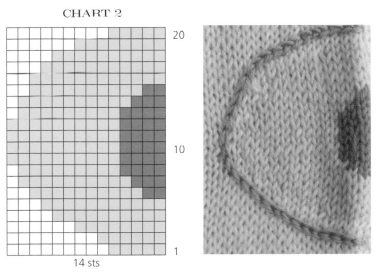

20

10

1

14 sts

CHART 3

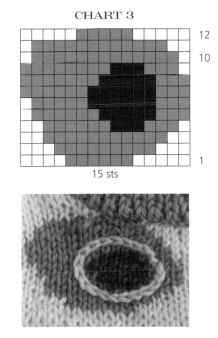

12

10

1

15 sts

COLOR KEY

☐ A ☐ B ◼ C ◼ D ☐ E

97

31

Eyelet Mock Turtleneck

This pullover is so full of flattering and fashionable design elements,
you'll want to make a big one for yourself!

DESIGNED BY CAROLYN NOYES

Sizes
Instructions are written for size
3 months (6 months, 12 months).
Shown in size 6 months.

Knitted Measurements
Chest 17½ (20, 22½)"/19 (51, 57)cm
Length 9½ (10½, 11½)"/24 (26.5, 29)cm
Upper arm 7 (8, 9)"/18 (20.5, 23)cm

Materials
■ 2 (2, 3) 1¾oz/50g skeins (each approx
229yd/210m) of Cascade Yarns
Cherub Baby Multis (nylon acrylic) in
#504 ballerina

■ Two size 5 (3.75mm) circular needles,
16"/41cm long, *or size to obtain gauge*

■ One set (5) size 5 (3.75mm) double-
pointed needles (dpns)

■ Stitch holders, stitch markers

Eyelet Pattern
(multiple of 8 sts)
Rnd 1 Knit.
Rnd 2 *K2, ssk, yo, k1, yo, k2tog, k1;
rep from * around.
Rnd 3 Knit.
Rnd 4 *K3, yo, S2KP, yo, k2; rep
from * around.

Rnd 5 Knit.
Rnd 6 Rep rnd 2.
Rnds 7–9 Knit.
Rnd 10 *K1, yo, k2tog, k3, ssk, yo;
rep from * around.
Rnd 11 Knit.
Note At beg of rnd 12 only, work as foll:
remove rnd marker, sl last st worked on
rnd 11 to LH needle (this st becomes the
first st of the "sl 2" that begs rnd 12).
When S2KP is completed, sl the resulting
1 st to LH needle, place marker back on
RH needle, then sl st back to RH needle
and resume pat with the yo.
Rnd 12 *S2KP, yo, k5, yo; rep
from * around.
Rnd 13 Knit.
Rnd 14 Rep rnd 10.
Rnds 15 and 16 Knit.
Rep rnds 1–16 for eyelet pat.

Notes
1) Body and sleeves are worked in the
rnd separately and joined when working
the yoke.
2) Yoke is worked in the rnd to front
neck shaping, then is worked back and
forth using two circular needles.
3) When shaping in eyelet pat, if there
are not enough sts to work a
compensating dec, do not work the yo.
4) When working back and forth in

eyelet pat, all odd-numbered (WS) rows
are purled.

Sleeves
With dpns, cast on 32 (40, 48) sts,
dividing sts evenly over 4 needles. Join,
being careful not to twist sts, and place
marker (pm) for beg of rnd. Work 12
rnds in garter st (k 1 rnd, p 1 rnd).
Work 2 rnds in St st (k every rnd). Work
rnds 1–6 of eyelet pat. Work even in in
St st for 4 rnds.
Next (inc) rnd K1, M1, k to last st, M1,
k1—2 sts inc'd.
Rep inc rnd every 6th (8th, 10th)
rnd 4 (3, 2) times more. Work even on 42
(48, 54) sts until piece measures 6
(6½, 7)"/15 (16.5, 18)cm from beg, end
last rnd 2 (3, 4) sts before marker.
Next rnd Bind off 4 (6, 8) sts for
underarm, k to end. Place rem 38
(42, 46) sts on st holder. Set aside.

Body
With circular needle, cast on 104 (120,
136) sts. Join, being careful not to twist
sts, and pm for beg of rnd. Work 12 rnds
in garter st. Knit 2 rnds. Work in eyelet
pat until piece measures approx 6½
(7, 7½)"/16.5 (18, 19)cm from beg, end
on rnd 7 or 15, and 2 (3, 4) sts before
beg-of-rnd marker.

Gauge
24 sts and 32 rnds to 4"/10cm over eyelet pat using size 5 (3.75mm) needle. *Take time to check gauge.*

Eyelet Mock Turtleneck

Next rnd Bind off 4 (6, 8) sts (left underarm), k until there are 48 (54, 60) sts on RH needle for front, bind off next 4 (6, 8) sts (right underarm), k rem 48 (54, 60) sts for back—96 (108, 120) sts.

JOIN BODY AND SLEEVES

Next rnd With circular needle, k 38 (42, 46) sts from first sleeve holder (left sleeve), pm, k next 48 (54, 60) sts on needle (front), pm, k 38 (42, 46) sts from 2nd sleeve holder (right sleeve), pm, k rem 48 (54, 60) sts on needle (back)— 172 (192, 212) sts. Join and pm for beg of rnds. Cont with rnd 10 or 1 of eyelet pat on front and back, and St st on sleeves. Work raglan shaping as foll:

Rnd 1 (dec) *K1, S2KP, work to 4 sts before next marker, k3tog, k1, sl marker, k1, work to 1 st before next marker, k1, sl marker; rep from * around once more— 164 (184, 204) sts; no sts dec on front/back and 4 sts dec on each sleeve; 48 (54, 60) sts for front/back and 34 (38, 42) sts for each sleeve.

Rnd 2 and all even-numbered rnds Work even in pats.

Rnd 3 (dec) *K1, S2KP, work to 4 sts of next marker, k3tog, k1, sl marker, k1, ssk, work to 3 sts of next of marker, k2tog, k1, sl marker; rep from * around once more—152 (172, 192) sts; 2 sts dec on front/back and 4 sts dec on each sleeve;

46 (52, 58) sts for front/back and 30 (34, 38) sts for each sleeve.

Rnd 5 (dec) *K1, ssk, work to 3 sts before next marker, k2tog, k1, sl marker, k1, work to 1 st before next of marker, k1, sl marker; rep from * around once more—148 (168, 188) sts; no sts dec on front/back and 2 sts dec on each sleeve; 46 (52, 58) sts for front/back and 28 (32, 36) sts for each sleeve.

Rnd 7 (dec) *K1, ssk, work to 3 sts before next marker, k2tog, k1, sl marker; rep from * around 3 times more—2 sts dec on front/back and 2 sts dec on each sleeve; 44 (50, 56) sts for front/back and 26 (30, 34) sts for each sleeve.

Rnd 9 (dec) Rep rnd 5—136 (156, 176) sts; 44 (50, 56) sts for front/back and 24 (28, 32) sts for each sleeve.

Rnd 11 (dec) Rep rnd 7—128 (148, 168) sts; 42 (48, 54) sts for front/back and 22 (26, 30) sts for each sleeve.

Rnd 13 (dec) Rep rnd 5—124 (144, 164) sts; 42 (48, 54) sts for front/back and 20 (24, 28) sts for each sleeve.

Rnd 15 (dec) *K1, ssk, work to 3 sts before next marker, k2tog, k1, sl marker; rep from * around 3 times more—116 (136, 156) sts; 40 (46, 52) sts for front/back and 18 (22, 26) sts for each sleeve.

Rnd 16 Work even around. Rep last 2 rnds 1 (3, 5) times more—108 (112, 116)

sts; 38 (40, 42) sts for front/back and 16 sts for each sleeve.

FRONT NECK SHAPING

Cont raglan shaping and beg front neck shaping as foll:

Next (dec) rnd *K1, ssk, work to 3 sts before next marker, k2tog, k1, sl marker*, k1, ssk, work until there are 25 (27, 29) sts on RH needle after last marker on RH needle, place last 14 (16, 18) sts worked on st holder for front neck, work to 3 sts before next marker, k2tog, k1, sl marker, rep from * to * twice more—86 (88, 90) sts. You will now be working back and forth on two circular needles.

Next row (WS) Purl. Cont raglan shaping every RS row as established 4 times more. AT THE SAME TIME, bind off 3 sts from each neck edge once, then 1 st 3 times, end with a WS row—42 (44, 46) sts; 2 sts for front, 28 (30, 32) sts for back and 6 sts for each sleeve. Leave sts on needle.

NECKBAND

With RS facing, using circular needle (and dropping markers as you work), pick up and k 7 sts evenly spaced along left front neck edge, k 14 (16, 18) sts from front neck holder, pick up and k 7 sts evenly spaced along right front neck edge, k rem 42 (44, 46) sts on needle—70 (74, 78) sts. Pm for beg of rnds. Beg with a purl rnd, cont in garter st for 1½"/4cm, end with a purl rnd. Bind off loosely knitwise.

Finishing

Lightly block piece to measurements. Sew underarm seams. ∎

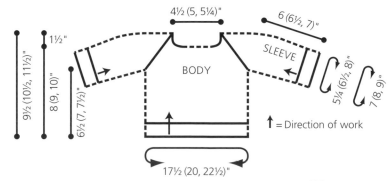

4½ (5, 5¼)" 6 (6½, 7)"

1½"

9½ (10½, 11½)" 8 (9, 10)" 6½ (7, 7½)"

SLEEVE

BODY

5¼ (6½, 8)" 7 (8, 9)"

↑ = Direction of work

17½ (20, 22½)"

100

32

Dainty Dress

A lace border at the bottom and picot at the neck, along with a little sparkle, make this a frock fit for any occasion.

DESIGNED BY CAROL J. SULCOSKI

Sizes
Instructions are written for size 3 months (6 months, 12 months). Shown in size 12 months.

Knitted Measurements
Chest 20 (21, 22)"/51 (53, 56)cm
Length 12 (13¼, 14)"/30.5 (33.5, 35.5)cm

Materials
■ 1 (2, 2) 3½oz/100g skeins (each approx 240yd/220m) of Cascade Yarns *Cherub Aran Sparkle* (nylon/acrylic/metallic) in #207 striking purple

■ Size 8 (5mm) circular needle, 24"/60cm long, *or size to obtain gauge*

■ Size 7 (4.5mm) circular needle, 16"/40cm long

■ Spare size 8 (5mm) needle for 3-needle bind-off

■ Stitch markers, stitch holders

Cable Cast-On
Insert tip of RH needle between the next 2 sts on LH needle, wrap yarn knitwise and draw up a loop, place loop on LH needle—1 st cast on.

3-Needle Bind-Off
1) Hold right sides of pieces together on two needles. Insert 3rd needle knitwise into first st of each needle, and wrap yarn knitwise.
2) Knit these two sts together, and slip them off the needles. *Knit the next two sts together in the same manner.
3) Slip first st on 3rd needle over 2nd st and off needle. Rep from * in step 2 across row until all sts are bound off.

Picot Bind-Off
*Cast on 1 st using cable cast-on method, bind off 3 sts, place loop from bind-off on LH needle; rep from * until all sts have been bound off. Fasten off last st.

Lace Border
(multiple of 11 sts)
Rnd 1 *Ssk, k3tbl, yo, k1, yo, k3tbl, k2tog; rep from * around.
Rnd 2 and all even-numbered rows through row 8 Knit.
Rnd 3 *Ssk, k2tbl, yo, k1, yo, ssk, yo, k2tbl, k2tog; rep from * around.
Rnd 5 *Ssk, k1tbl, yo, k1, yo, [ssk, yo] twice, k1tbl, k2tog; rep from * around.
Rnd 7 *Ssk, yo, k1, [yo, ssk] 3 times, yo, k2tog; rep from * around.
Rnds 9 and 10 *K1, p1, k7, p1, k1; rep from * around.

Gauge
18 sts and 24 rnds to 4"/10cm over St st using larger needle.
Take time to check gauge.

Note
Dress is worked in the round from the lower edge to the armholes in one piece.

Dress
With larger needle, cast on 99 (99, 110) sts. Join, being careful not to twist sts, and place marker (pm) for beg of rnd. Work rows 1–10 of lace border.
Rep row 10 of lace border pat until piece measures 6½ (7½, 8)"/16.5 (19, 20.5)cm from beg.
Next (dec) rnd Knit, dec 9 (3, 10) sts evenly around—90 (96, 100) sts.
Purl 2 rnds, knit 6 rnds.

DIVIDE FOR FRONT AND BACK
Next rnd K42 (44, 48), bind off next 6 (8, 8) sts, k to last 3 (4, 4) sts, bind off next 6 (8, 8) sts, removing marker. Place last 39 (40, 42) sts worked on st holder for front.
Working on 39 (40, 42) sts for back, cont to shape armhole as foll:
Next (dec) row (RS) K1, ssk, k to last 3 sts, k2tog, k1—2 sts dec'd.
Next row (WS) Purl.
Rep last 2 rows twice more—33 (34, 36) sts.
Work even in St st until armhole measures 4½ (4¾, 5)"/11.5 (12, 12.5)cm. Place sts on a st holder.

FRONT
Place front sts on needle, ready to work a RS row. Shape armhole as for back. Work even until armhole measures 2½ (2¾, 3)"/6.5 (7, 7.5)cm, end with a WS row.

SHAPE NECK
Next row (RS) K10, turn.
Next row (WS) P10.

Next (dec) row K to last 3 sts, k2tog, k1—1 st dec'd.
Cont in St st, rep dec row every other row twice more—7 sts.
Work even on rem sts for shoulder until armhole measures same as back. Place sts on st holder.
Rejoin yarn to center sts, k13 (14, 16) and place these sts on st holder for front neck.
Cont on rem 10 sts for 2nd shoulder as foll:
Next row (RS) K10, turn.
Next row (WS) P10.
Next (dec) row K1, ssk, k to end—1 st dec'd.
Cont in St st, rep dec row every other row twice more—7 sts.
Work even on rem sts for shoulder until armhole measures same as back.

Finishing
Carefully turn piece inside out and join front and back shoulders using 3-needle bind-off method. Turn dress right side out.

NECK TRIM
With smaller needle, beg at back left shoulder, pick up and k 10 sts along neck edge of shoulder strap, k 13 (14, 16) front neck sts, pick up and k 10 sts along neck edge of 2nd shoulder strap, k 19 (20, 22) back sts, pm for beg of rnd—42 (44, 48) sts.
Purl 1 rnd. Bind off using picot bind-off method.

ARMHOLE TRIM
With smaller needle and RS facing, pick up and k 45 (48, 50) sts, pm for beg of rnd.
Purl 1 rnd. Bind off knitwise. ∎

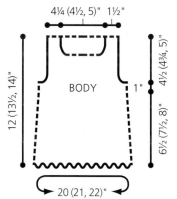

4¼ (4½, 5)" 1½"

12 (13½, 14)"

BODY

1"

4½ (4¾, 5)"

6½ (7½, 8)"

20 (21, 22)"

33

Bow Dress & Pants

A Peter Pan collar, bows, tiny cables, and lace make this outfit
a little girl's dream design.

DESIGNED BY SANDI PROSSER

Sizes
Instructions are written for size 6 months (12 months). Shown in size 6 months.

Knitted Measurements
DRESS
Chest 20½ (21½)"/52 (54.5)cm
Length 12 (13)"/30.5 (33)cm
Upper arm 9 (9½)"/23 (24)cm

PANTS
Length of leg 7½ (8½)"/19 (21.5)cm
Hips 19½ (20½)"/49.5 (52)cm

Materials
■ 3 1¾oz/50g skeins (each approx 180yd/165m) of Cascade Yarns *Cherub DK* (nylon/acrylic) in #9 ecru (A)

■ 1 skein in #11 key lime (B)

■ 2 skeins in #526 tropical (C)

■ One pair each sizes 3 and 4 (3.25 and 4.5mm) needles *or size to obtain gauge*

■ Stitch holders, stitch markers

■ Cable needle (cn)

■ 1 button

■ ½yd (.5m) of 1"/2.5cm-wide elastic

Stitch Glossary
5-st LC Sl 3 sts to cn and hold to *front*, k2, k3 from cn.

Cable Panel
(worked over 5 sts)
Row 1 (RS) Knit.
Row 2 and all WS rows Purl.
Row 3 5-st LC.
Row 5 Knit.
Row 6 Purl.
Rep rows 1–6 for cable panel.

Lace Pattern
(multiple of 10 sts plus 3)
Row 1 (RS) K2, *k4, yo, ssk, k4; rep from * to last st, k1.
Row 2 and all WS rows Purl.
Row 3 K2, *k2, k2tog, yo, k1, yo, ssk, k3; rep from * to last st, k1.
Row 5 K2, *k1, k2tog, yo, k3, yo, ssk, k2; rep from * to last st, k1.
Row 7 K2, *k2tog, yo, k5, yo, ssk, k1; rep from * to last st, k1.
Row 9 K1, k2tog, *yo, k7, yo, SK2P; rep from * to last st, end last rep ssk instead of S2KP; k1.
Row 10 Purl.
Rep rows 1–10 for lace pat.

Dress Back
With smaller needles and A, cast on
123 (143) sts. Beg with a WS row, knit 3 rows. Change to larger needle and cont in lace pat until piece measures 7 (7½)"/18 (19)cm from beg.
Next row (RS) K6 (4), *k2tog; rep from * to last 5 (3) sts, k5 (3)—67 (75) sts. Bind off all sts purlwise.

BODICE
With smaller needles and A, working from the RS, pick up and k 67 (75) sts along the bound-off edge**. Beg with a purl row, work in St st for 1"/2.5cm from the pick-up row.

SHAPE ARMHOLE
Bind off 3 sts at beg of next 2 rows. Dec 1 st each side of next 3 (5) rows, then dec 1 st each side every RS row 3 times—49 (53) sts. Work even until bodice measures 3 (3½)"/7.5 (9)cm.

DIVIDE FOR NECK OPENING
Next row (RS) K26 (28), turn, leaving rem sts for left back unworked.
Row 1 (WS) K3, p to end.
Row 2 Knit.
Rep these 2 rows for 1½"/4cm.
Buttonhole row (RS) K to last 2 sts, yo, k2tog.
Work even until piece measures 5 (5½)"/12.5 (14)cm from pick-up row.

Gauge
26 sts and 34 rows to 4"/10cm over St st using larger needles. *Take time to check gauge.*

Pattern for
Just-Right
Ribbed Booties
is on page 24.

Bow Dress & Pants

Next row (RS) Bind off 11 (13) sts for shoulder and place rem 15 sts on st holder for right back.

Return to the sts for left back, and from the RS, cast on 3 sts, k to end—26 (28) sts. Work as for first side with garter trim in reverse (end of WS rows) and without the buttonhole.

Front

Work as for back to **.

Inc row (WS) P15 (17), k1, [p1, M1 p-st] twice, p1, k1, p11 (13), k1, [p1, M1 p-st] twice, p1, k1, p11 (13), k1, [p1, M1 p-st] twice, p1, k1, p15 (17)—73 (81) sts.

BEGIN CABLE PAT

Row 1 (RS) K15 (17), [p1, work row 1 of cable pat over next 5 sts, p1, k11 (13)] twice, p1, work row 1 of cable pat over next 5 sts, p1, k15 (17).
Work even in pat as established until piece measures 1"/2.5cm from pick-up row.

SHAPE ARMHOLE

Work as for back armhole—55 (59) sts. Work even until bodice measures 3 (3½)"/7.5 (9)cm.

SHAPE NECK

Next row (RS) Work 20 (22) sts, join a 2nd ball of yarn and bind off 15 sts, work to end.
Working both sides at once, dec 1 st at each neck edge every row on the next 4 rows, then dec 1 st every RS row 3 times—13 (15) sts rem each side. Work even until armhole measures same as back, end with a RS row. On the next row, dec 2 sts over each set of cables, then bind off 11 (13) sts each side for shoulders.

Sleeves

With smaller needles and A, cast on 43 (45) sts. Knit 2 rows.

Next row (RS) Knit, inc 15 (17) sts evenly spaced—58 (62) sts. Change to larger needles. Then, beg with a WS (purl) row, work in St st until piece measures 1"/2.5cm from beg.

Shape Cap

Bind off 3 sts at beg of next 2 rows. Dec 1 st each side of next 3 rows, then dec 1 st each side every RS row 10 (12) times—26 sts. Purl 1 row.
Next row (RS) K1, [k2tog] 12 times, k1. Bind off rem 14 sts.

Finishing

Lightly block pieces to measurements. Sew shoulder seams. Sew right back band overlapping left back band at the base. Sew on button.

Collar

RIGHT HALF
Working from the WS with B, work 15 sts from right back holder, pick up and k 17 sts from shaped neck edge, then pick up and k 8 sts to center front neck—40 sts. Knit 3 rows.

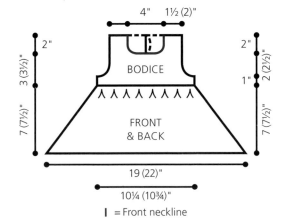

9¾ (10¼)"
2"
6"
RIGHT LEG
7½ (8½)"
7½ (8)"
8½ (9¼)"

9 (9½)"
3 (3½)"
SLEEVE
1"
6½ (7)"

4" 1½ (2)"
2" 2"
3 (3½)" 2 (2½)"
BODICE
1"
7 (7½)" 7 (7½)"
FRONT & BACK
19 (22)"
10¼ (10¾)"
I = Front neckline

Next row (WS) [K4, M1] 9 times, k4—49 sts.
Work 9 rows in garter st.
Next row [K5, M1] 8 times, k6, k2tog, k1—56 sts.
Next row Knit.
Next (dec) row K to last 3 sts, k2tog, k1.
Rep last 2 rows twice more—53 sts.
Bind off.

LEFT HALF
Work as for right half, reversing shaping.

Bows (make 3)
With smaller needle and B, cast on 11 sts.
Knit 10 rows. Bind off.
Cut a length of B and wrap around center, pulling tightly to create the bow. Sew bows in place above each cable. Set in sleeves. Sew side and sleeve seams.

Pants
RIGHT LEG
**With smaller needles and C, cast on 49 (53) sts. Work 5 rows in garter st, inc 7 sts evenly across last WS row—56 (60) sts. Change to larger needles. Then, beg with a knit row, work in St st, inc 1 st each side of the 5th row, then every 6th row 8 times more—74 (78) sts.
Work even until piece measures 7½ (8½)"/19 (21.5)cm from beg. Place marker in each end of last row.

SHAPE CROTCH
Bind off 2 sts at beg of next 2 rows.
Next (dec) row (RS) K1, k2tog, k to the last 3 sts, SKP, k1—2 sts dec'd.
Rep dec row every other row twice more—64 (68) sts**.
Work even until piece measures 6"/15cm from the markers, end with a RS row.

SHAPE BACK
Row 1 (WS) P18, turn.
Row 2 and all RS rows Sl 1, k to end.
Row 3 P24, turn.
Row 5 P30, turn.
Row 7 P36, turn.
Row 9 Purl across all sts to end of row.
Work even for 7 rows.
Next (turning) row (WS) Knit.
Change to smaller needles and beg with a k row, work in St st for 8 rows.
Bind off.

LEFT LEG
Work same as right leg from ** to **.
Work even until piece measures 6"/15cm from the markers, end with a WS row.

SHAPE BACK
Row 1 (RS) K18, turn. Then, reversing the WS (purl) and RS (knit) rows, cont to work as for right leg.

Finishing
Block lightly to measurements. Sew leg inseams from cast-on edge to markers. Sew crotch seam. Cut elastic to desired finished measurements. Fold waistband to WS along fold line and stitch in place, leaving an opening for the elastic. Thread elastic length through waistband opening and secure ends in place. Sew waistband closed. ∎

Zebra Hat

What's black and white and cute all over? This delightful hat, complete with flowing mane and perky ears

DESIGNED BY AMY BAHRT

Size
Instructions are written for size 6–24 months.

Knitted Measurements
Head circumference 16"/40.5cm
Length 7"/18cm
Note that border of hat will roll approx ½"/1.5cm.

Materials
■ 1 3½oz/100g skein (each approx 240yd/220m) of Cascade Yarns *Cherub Aran* (nylon/acrylic) each in #40 black (A) and #01 white (B)

■ One pair size 7 (4.5mm) needles *or size to obtain gauge*

■ Size G/6 (4mm) crochet hook

Hat
With A, cast on 72 sts. Work 10 rows in St st (k on RS, p on WS) for border. Cont in St st, work 2 rows A, 2 rows B for stripe pat until hat measures 5½"/14cm from beg, end with a RS row.

SHAPE CROWN
Set up row (WS) Cont in stripe pat, [p8, place marker] 8 times, p8.
Next (dec) row (RS) [K to marker, k2tog] 9 times around—9 sts dec'd sts. Cont in stripe pat to end of hat, rep dec row every other row 3 times more—36 sts. Work 1 row even.
Next (dec) row (RS) [K2tog] 18 times across.
Break yarn, leaving a long tail. Thread tail through rem 18 sts and pull tightly to close. Sew back seam.

Finishing
EAR
With A, cast on 3 sts. Work even in St st for 2 rows.
Inc 1 st each side every other row 3 times—9 sts.
Work 6 rows even.
Dec 1 st each side every other row 3 times—3 sts.

Purl 1 row. K3tog. Fasten off. With crochet hook, work 1 rnd of slip st around ear. Fold in half and sew to side of head, approx 6"/15cm from beg. Rep for 2nd ear.

MANE
With A, make a 4"/10cm pompom and attach to top of hat. Cut 36 strands of A, each approx 5½"/14cm long. Holding 2 strands tog, fold in half. With crochet hook, draw folded loop through st at center back seam, draw ends of strand through loop and tighten to form fringe. Rep along back seam of hat, from pompom to just above border. ■

Gauge
18 sts and 26 rows to 4"/10cm over St st using size 7 (4.5mm) needles.
Take time to check gauge.

Stripy Puffy Pants

A playful pompom tie is a cute finishing touch on a pair of pants
with an elastic band and roomy fit for maximum comfort.

DESIGNED BY GALINA CARROLL

Sizes
Instructions are written for size 3 months
(6 months, 12 months). Shown in size
12 months.

Knitted Measurements
Waist 18 (20, 21)"/45.5 (51, 53.5)cm
Length below waist 10¾ (11½,
12¾)"/27 (29, 32.5)cm
Hips 28 (30, 32)"/71 (76, 81)cm

Materials
■ 1 3½oz/100g skein (each approx
240yd/220m) of Cascade Yarns *Cherub
Aran* (nylon/acrylic) each in #06 baby
peach (A), #14 melon (B), #19 geranium
(C), #22 rouge (D), and #25 ruby (E)

■ Size 8 (5mm) circular needle,
24"/60cm long, *or size to obtain gauge*

■ One set (5) size 8 (5mm) double-
pointed needles (dpns)

■ 4 stitch markers

■ 19½ (20½, 21½)"/49.5 (52, 54.5)cm
elastic length, ¾"/2cm wide

Twisted Cord
1) Cut 2 lengths of of yarn 3 times the
desired finished length and knot them
about 1"/2.5cm from each end.
2) Insert a pencil or knitting needle
through each end of the strands. Turn
the strands clockwise until they are
tightly twisted.
3) Keeping the strands taut, fold the
piece in half. Remove the needles and
allow the cords to twist onto themselves.

3-Needle Bind-Off
1) Hold right sides of pieces together on
2 needles. Insert 3rd needle knitwise into
first st of each needle, and wrap yarn
knitwise.
2) Knit these 2 sts together, and slip
them off the needles. *Knit the next 2 sts
together in the same manner.
3) Slip first st on 3rd needle over 2nd st
and off needle. Rep from * in step 2
across row until all sts are bound off.

Note
Pants are worked from waist to cuff.

K1, P1 Rib
(over an even number of sts)
Rnd 1 *K1, p1; rep from * to end.
Rep rnd 1 for k1, p1 rib.

Pants
WAISTBAND
With A and circular needle, cast on
112 (120, 128) sts.
Next row (RS) *K1, p1; rep from
* to end. Join, being careful not to
twist sts, and place marker (pm) for
beg of rnd. Work in k1, p1 rib for
2¼"/5.5cm. Work in St st (k every rnd)
for 3 (3¼, 3½)"/7.5(8, 9)cm. Work 1
rnd E. With B, work for 3¼ (3½, 3¾)"/
8 (9, 9.5)cm. Work 1 rnd E.
Work 5 (6, 7) rnds B.

DIVIDE FOR LEGS
Next rnd K16 (18, 20) and place these
sts on st holder for crotch, pm, k40 (42,
44) for leg, k16 (18, 20) and place these
sts on st holder for crotch, pm, k40 (42,
44) sts for 2nd leg.
Carefully turn piece inside out so that
RS of crotch sts are tog, and graft sts tog
using Kitchener st or 3-needle bind-off.
Turn piece RS out.
Place 40 (42, 44) leg sts evenly on 4
dpns, pm for beg of rnd. Work 1 rnd E.
Work 1 rnd C.

SHAPE LEG
Next (dec) rnd Cont with C, k2tog,
work to last 2 sts, SKP—38 (40, 42) sts.

Gauge
16 sts and 20 rnds to 4"/10cm over St st using size 8 (5mm) needles.
Take time to check gauge.

Work 1 rnd even. Rep dec rnd—36 (38, 40) sts.
Work 0 (0, 1) rnd even. Knit 1 rnd E, knit 1 rnd D.
Cont with D, rep dec rnd once—34 (36, 38) sts.
Work 1 rnd even.
Rep dec rnd once more—32 (34, 36) sts.
Work 0 (0, 1) rnd even. Knit 1 rnd E.
Cont with E, work in k1, p1 rib for 1"/2.5cm. Bind off in rib loosely.
Rep for 2nd leg.

Finishing

Fold ribbed waistband in half. From WS, sew cast-on edge to first St st rnd, leaving 1"/2.5cm opening for elastic. Cut elastic to measure ½"/1.5cm longer than desired waist. Insert elastic through opening and draw through waistband. Being careful not to twist band, sew ends of elastic tog and sew the waistband opening closed. With E, make 2 twisted cords, 8"/20cm long and 12"/30.5cm long. With E, make a 2"/5cm pompom and attach to 8"/20.5cm cord. Make a 1½"/3.5cm pompom and attach to 12"/30.5cm cord. Pass end of each cord through to WS of pant front, just below waistband, about 1"/2.5cm apart. Tie ends in knot on WS of front to secure, then again on RS. ∎

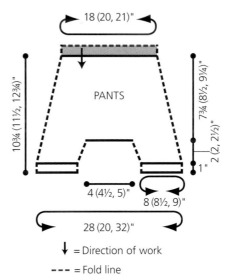

18 (20, 21)"

PANTS

10¾ (11½, 12¾)"

7¾ (8½, 9¼)"

2 (2, 2½)"

1"

4 (4½, 5)"

8 (8½, 9)"

28 (20, 32)"

↓ = Direction of work

- - - = Fold line

36

Fair Isle Onesie

An allover colorwork pattern adds visual depth to a super-warm button-up onesie.

DESIGNED BY GAYLE BUNN

Sizes
Instructions are written for size
3 months (6 months, 12 months). Shown in size 3 months.

Knitted Measurements
Chest (closed) 17¾ (19½, 21)"/45 (49.5, 53.5)cm
Length 20½ (22, 23½)"/52 (56, 59.5)cm
Upper arm 7 (8, 9)"/18 (20.5, 23)cm

Materials
■ 1 3½oz/100g skein (each approx 240yd/220m) of Cascade Yarns *Cherub DK* (nylon/acrylic) each in #24 chocolate (A), #09 ecru (B), #41 blue mirage (C), #35 taupe (D), and #40 black (C)

■ One pair each sizes 3 and 4 (3.25 and 3.5mm) needles *or size to obtain gauge*

■ Two size 4 (3.5mm) circular needles, 16"/41cm long

■ Stitch holders, stitch markers

■ Thirteen ⁹⁄₁₆"/13mm buttons

Notes
1) Row gauge is as important as stitch gauge to ensure matching chart pat accurately.
2) Legs and sleeves are made separately and worked back and forth in rows.
3) Body is worked in rnds to placket opening, then worked back and forth in rows using two circular needles.
4) When working raglan shaping, use a separate strand of C for each side of raglan edge border.

K1, P1 Rib
(over an odd number of sts)
Row 1 (RS) K1, *p1, k1; rep from * to end.
Row 2 P1, *k1, p1; rep from * to end.
Rep rows 1 and 2 for k1, p1 rib.

Onesie
LEGS
With smaller needles and A, cast on 47 (49, 51) sts. Work in k1, p1 rib for 8 rows, inc 1 (3, 5) sts evenly spaced across last row and end with a WS row—48 (52, 56) sts. Change to larger needles and St st (k on RS, p on WS).

BEG CHART PAT
Next row (RS) Beg chart on row 1 (9, 3) and work 4-st rep 12 (13, 14) times across. Cont to foll chart in this way through row 16, then rep rows 1–16 for chart pat. AT THE SAME TIME, when 8 rows have been completed, end with a WS row. Inc 1 st each side on next row, then every 6th row 4 (5, 6) times more, working new sts into chart pat. Work even on 58 (64, 70) sts until piece measures approx 7 (7½, 8)"/18 (19, 20.5)cm from beg, end with a row 11 (5, 3). Place sts on holder.

Gauge
28 sts to 4"/10cm and 32 rows to 4½"/11.5cm over St st and chart pat using larger needles.
Take time to check gauge.

Body

JOIN LEGS

Next rnd With RS facing and circular needle, place first 29 (32, 35) sts from one leg holder on RH needle, pm for beg of rnd, join E (D, C), k next 29 (32, 35) leg sts from holder, cast on 8 sts (front crotch), k 58 (64, 70) sts from 2nd leg holder, cast on 8 sts (back crotch), k 29 (32, 35) sts rem on needle—132 (144, 156) sts. Cont with rnd 13 (7, 5), work around in St st (k every rnd) until piece measures approx 3 (3, 3¼)"/7.5 (7.5, 8)cm from crotch cast-on, end with a rnd 1 (11, 11).

WAIST SHAPING

Next (dec) rnd With B (E, E), [k31 (34, 37), k2tog] 4 times—128 (140, 152) sts. Cont with rnd 3 (13, 13), work even through rnd 11 (5, 5).
Next (dec) rnd With E (D, D), [k30 (33, 36), k2tog] 4 times—124 (136, 148) sts. Cont with rnd 13 (7, 7), work even for 4 (8, 10) rnds, end with rnd 16 (14, 16). Piece should measure approx 5 (5½, 6)"/12.5 (14, 15)cm from crotch cast-on. Cont with rnd 1 (15, 1), work as foll:

PLACKET OPENING

Next rnd Work across first 27 (30, 33) sts, bind off center 8 sts, work to end of rnd—116 (128, 140) sts. Break yarn. Place next 27 (30, 33) sts on RH needle, turn. Rejoin yarn to work row 2 (16, 2) on WS. You will now be working back and forth in rows using two circular needles. Work even foll chart until piece measures approx 9 (9½, 10)"/23 (24, 25.5)cm from crotch cast-on, end with row 12 (10, 12).

DIVIDE FOR FRONTS AND BACK

Cont to foll chart with row 13 (11, 13) and work as foll:
Next row (RS) Work across first 25 (28, 30) sts (right front), bind off next 4 (4, 6) sts (right underarm), work across next 58 (64, 68) sts (back), bind off next 4 (4, 6) sts (left underarm), work across rem 25 (28, 30) sts (left front). Keeping continuity of chart pat as established, work as foll:

LEFT FRONT

Change to larger straight needles. Work next chart row.

RAGLAN AND NECK SHAPING

Row (dec) 1 (RS) With C, k2, working chart pat, k2tog, work to end.
Row (dec) 2 Work chart pat to last 4 sts, end p2tog, with C, p2.
Row (dec) 3 Rep row 1.
Row 4 Work chart pat to last 2 sts, end with C, p2.
Rep last 4 rows once more—19 (22, 24) sts.
Row (dec) 5 With C, k2, working chart pat, k2tog, work to end.
Row 6 Work chart pat to last 2 sts, end with C, p2.
Rep last 2 rows 2 (4, 6) times more, then row 5 once—15 (16, 16) sts.
Cont raglan shaping and beg neck shaping as foll:
Next row (WS) Bind off first 3 (4, 4) sts, work to last 2 sts, with C, p2—12 sts.
Row (dec) 1 (RS) With C, k2, working chart pat, k2tog, work to last 2 sts, k2tog.
Row 2 Work chart pat to last 2 sts, end with C, p2.
Rep last 2 rows 3 times more—4 sts.
Row (dec) 3 (RS) With C only, k2, k2tog—3 sts.

Row 4 With C, p3.
Row (dec) 5 With C, k1, k2tog—2 sts.
Row 6 With C, p2.
Row (dec) 7 With C, k2tog. Fasten off last st.

Back

With WS facing and larger straight needles, join yarn and work across 58 (64, 68) sts, end with a WS row.

RAGLAN SHAPING

Row (dec) 1 (RS) With C, k2, working chart pat, k2tog, work to last 4 sts, end ssk, with C, k2.
Row (dec) 2 With C, p2, working chart pat, p2tog tbl, work to last 4 sts, end p2tog, with C, p2.
Row (dec) 3 Rep row 1.
Row 4 With C, p2, work chart pat to last 2 sts, end with C, p2.
Rep last 4 rows once more—46 (52, 56) sts.
Row (dec) 5 With C, k2, working chart pat, k2tog, work to last 4 sts, end ssk, with C, k2.
Row 6 With C, p2, work chart pat to last 2 sts, end with C, p2.
Rep last 2 rows 9 (11, 13) times more—26 (28, 28) sts. Place sts on holder.

RIGHT FRONT

With WS facing and larger straight needles, join yarn and work across 27 (30, 33) sts.

Fair Isle Onesie

RAGLAN AND NECK SHAPING

Row (dec) 1 (RS) Work chart pat to last 4 sts, ssk, with CC, k2.

Row (dec) 2 With C, p2, working chart pat, p2tog tbl, work to end.

Row (dec) 3 Rep row 1.

Row 4 With C, p2, work chart pat to end.

Rep last 4 rows once more—19 (22, 24) sts.

Row (dec) 5 Work chart pat to last 4 sts, ssk, with CC, k2.

Row 6 With C, p2, work chart pat to end.

Rep last 2 rows 2 (4, 6) times more, end with a WS row—16 (17, 17) sts. Cont raglan shaping and beg neck shaping as foll:

Row (dec) 1 (RS) Bind off first 3 (4, 4) sts, work to last 4 sts, ssk, with C, p2—12 sts.

Row 2 With C, p2, work chart pat to end.

Row (dec) 3 Working chart pat, ssk, work to last 4 sts, ssk, with CC, k2.

Row 4 With C, p2, work chart pat to end.

Rep last 2 rows 3 times more—4 sts.

Row (dec) 3 (RS) With C only, ssk, k2—3 sts.

Row 4 With C, p3.

Row (dec) 5 With C, ssk, k1—2 sts.

Row 6 With C, p2.

Row (dec) 7 With C, ssk. Fasten off last st.

Sleeves

With smaller needles and A, cast on 39 (41, 45) sts. Work in k1, p1 rib for 8 rows, inc 5 (7, 7) sts evenly spaced across last row—44 (48, 52) sts. Change to larger needles and St st.

BEG CHART PAT

Next row (RS) Beg chart on row 9 (3, 1) and work 4-st rep 11 (12, 13) times across. Cont to foll chart in this way through row 16, then rep rows 1–16 for chart pat. AT THE SAME TIME, when 8 rows have been completed, end with a WS row. Inc 1 st each side on next row, then every 8th row 2 (3, 4) times more, working new sts into chart pat. Work even on 50 (56, 62) sts until piece measures approx 6 (6½, 7)"/15 (16.5, 18)cm from beg, end with row 12 (10, 12).

RAGLAN SHAPING

Keeping to chart pat as established, cont as foll:

Bind off 2 (2, 3) sts at beg of next 2 rows.

Row (dec) 1 (RS) With C, k2, working chart pat, k2tog, work to last 4 sts, end ssk, with C, k2.

Row (dec) 2 With C, p2, working chart pat, p2tog tbl, work to last 4 sts, end p2tog, with C, p2.

Row (dec) 3 Rep row 1.

Row 4 With C, p2, work chart pat to last 2 sts, end with C, p2.

Rep last 4 rows twice more—28 (34, 38) sts.

Row (dec) 5 With C, k2, working chart pat, k2tog, work to last 4 sts, end ssk, with C, k2.

Row 6 With C, p2, work chart pat to last 2 sts, end with C, p2.

Rep last 2 rows 7 (9, 11) times more—12 (14, 14) sts. Place sts on holder.

Finishing

Lightly block pieces to measurements. Sew sleeve seams. Set sleeves into raglan armholes.

NECKBAND

With RS facing, smaller needles, and A, pick up and k 13 sts evenly spaced along right front neck edge, k 12 (14, 14) sts from sleeve holder, dec 1 st in center, k 26 (28, 28) sts from back neck holder, dec 1 st in center, k 12 (14, 14) sts from sleeve holder, dec 1 st in center, pick up and k 13 sts evenly spaced along left front neck edge—73 (79, 79) sts. Beg with row 2, work in k1, p1 rib for 7 rows. Bind off loosely in rib.

BUTTON PLACKET

With RS facing, smaller needles, and A, pick up and k 47 sts evenly spaced across right front placket opening. Beg with row 2, work in k1, p1 rib for 9 rows. Bind off loosely in rib.

BUTTONHOLE PLACKET

With RS facing, smaller needles, and A, pick up and k 47 sts evenly spaced across left front placket opening. Beg with row 2, work in k1, p1 rib for 5 rows.

Next (buttonhole) row (RS) Work in rib over first 3 sts, *bind off next 2 sts, work in rib over next 11 sts; rep from * twice more, end bind off next 2 sts, work in rib over last 3 sts.

Next row Work in rib, casting on 2 sts over bound-off sts. Work in rib for 2 rows more. Bind off loosely in rib.

INSEAM BUTTON BAND

With RS facing, smaller needles, and A, pick up and k 55 (58, 61) sts evenly spaced along left back leg edge, 9 sts across back crotch edge, then 55 (58, 61) sts along right back leg edge—119 (125, 131) sts. Beg with row 2, work in k1, p1 rib for 7 rows. Bind off loosely in rib. Place markers for 9 buttons on inseam button band, with the first and last ³⁄₈"/1cm from bottom edge of each leg, one in center of crotch, and three more evenly spaced between right leg and left leg.

INSEAM BUTTONHOLE BAND

With RS facing, smaller needles, and A, pick up and k 55 (58, 61) sts evenly spaced along right front leg edge, 9 sts across front crotch edge, then 55 (58, 61) sts along left front leg edge—119 (125, 131) sts. Beg with row 2, work in k1, p1 rib for 3 rows.

Next (buttonhole) row (RS) *Work in rib to marker, bind off next 2 sts; rep from * 8 times more, work in rib to end.
Next row Work in rib, casting on 2 sts over bound-off sts. Work in rib for 2 rows more. Bind off loosely in rib. Sew on buttons. ∎

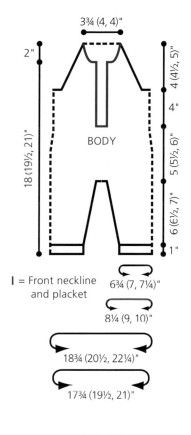

I = Front neckline and placket

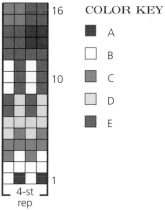

COLOR KEY

A
B
C
D
E

4-st rep

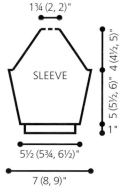

Giraffe Stroller Blanket

The parade of adorable giraffes on this fanciful intarsia blanket
will keep baby company and make everyone smile.

DESIGNED BY ANN FAITH

Knitted Measurements
Approximately 22 x 25"/56 x 63.5cm

Materials
■ 1¾oz/50g skeins (each approx
180yd/165m) of Cascade Yarns *Cherub
DK* (nylon/acrylic) in #9 ecru (A)

■ 1 skein each in #42 apple cinnamon (B)
and #51 yellow curry (C)

■ One pair size 6 (4mm) needles *or size
to obtain gauge*

■ Size F/5 (3.75mm) crochet hook

Note
The giraffes and the garter stitch borders
are worked on the sides using the intarsia
technique. Use separate bobbins or
lengths of yarn for each color section.
Do not carry colors across WS of work.

Blanket
With B, cast on 121 sts. Work in garter st
(k every row) for 1½"/4cm, end with a
WS row.
Next row (RS) With B, k9; with A, k to
last 9 sts, k9 B.
Next row (WS) With B, k9; with A, p to
last 9 sts, k9 B.

Cont in this manner, working center of
blanket in St st with A and garter stitch
borders each side with B, until piece
measures 17"/43cm from beg, end with
a WS row.

BEGIN CHART
Row 1 (RS) K9 B, k18 A, work chart row
over 17 sts, [k8 A, work chart row over
17 sts] twice, k18 A, k9 B.
Row 2 (WS) K9 B, p18 A, work chart row
over 17 sts, [p8 A, work chart row over
17 sts] twice, p18 A, k9 B.
Cont to work chart in this manner until
row 37 is complete.
Work center of blanket in St st with A
and garter stitch borders each side with
B, until piece measures 23½"/59.5cm
from beg, end with a WS row. With B,
work in garter st for 1½"/4cm. Bind off.

Finishing
EYES
With B, using chart for placement,
embroider French knot.

TAILS
Cut 3 strands of B, approx 3"/7.5cm
long for each tail. Make a braid approx
1"/2.5cm long and knot each end.
Attach to giraffes. ■

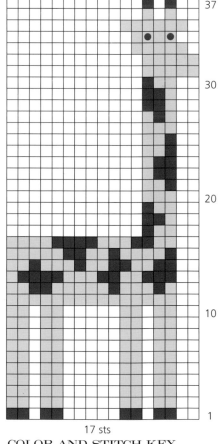

17 sts

COLOR AND STITCH KEY

□ A ■ B ▨ C ⦿ French knot

Gauge
19 sts and 26 rows to 4"/10cm over St st using size 7 (4.5mm) circular needle. *Take time to check gauge.*

Fancy Flared Jacket

The creative use of color emphasizes the sleeves, borders, and fun flared bottom of this delightful cardi.

DESIGNED BY LINDA MEDINA

Size
Instructions are written for size 12 months.

Knitted Measurements
Chest (closed) 22"/36cm
Length 13"/33cm
Upper arm 10"/25.5cm

Materials
■ 3 1¾oz/50g skeins (each approx 180yd/165m) of Cascade Yarns *Cherub DK* (nylon/acrylic) in #11 key lime (A)

■ 2 skeins in #17 grey (B)

■ Scrap yarn

■ One pair size 4 (3.5mm) needles *or size to obtain gauge*

■ Size 4 (3.5mm) circular needle, 16"/40cm long

■ One size 3 (3.25mm) needle for binding off in ribbing only

■ Five ⅜" (15mm) buttons

■ Stitch holders

■ Stitch markers

Corrugated Ribbing
(multiple of 4 sts)
Note Be sure to keep the stranding at the back slightly loose to keep the fabric flat.
Row 1 (WS) *K2 B, p2 A; rep from * to end.
Row 2 (RS) *K2 A, p2 B; rep from * to end.
Rows 3–6 Rep rows 1 and 2 twice. Cut B. With A and size 3 (3.25mm) needle, bind off.

Garter Stripe Pattern
(over any number of sts)
Beg with a RS row, knit 2 rows A, knit 2 rows B. Carry color not in use along side edge of work and pull new color from under old color to beg knitting.

Short Row
Wrap & Turn (w&t)
on RS row (on WS row)
1) Wyib (wyif), sl next st purlwise.
2) Move yarn between the needles to the front (back).
3) Sl the same st back to LH needle. Turn work. One st is wrapped.
4) When working the wrapped st, insert RH needle under the wrap and work it tog with the corresponding st on needle to hide or close wrap.

Note When working short rows that create the wedges in the skirt, it is not necessary to hide the wraps because they are hidden in the garter st.

3-Needle Bind-Off
1) Hold wrong sides of pieces together on 2 needles. Insert 3rd needle knitwise into first st of each needle, and wrap yarn knitwise.
2) Knit these 2 sts together, and slip them off the needles. *Knit the next 2 sts together in the same manner.
3) Slip first st on 3rd needle over 2nd st and off needle. Rep from * in step 2 across row until all sts are bound off.

Jacket
FLARE SKIRT
With size 4 (3.5mm) needles and A, cast on 42 sts.
With A, knit 30 rows.

SHORT ROW WEDGE 1
Row 1 (RS) K6 A, change to B and k36.
Row 2 K30 B, w&t.
Row 3 and all odd-numbered rows Knit.
Row 4 K24 B, w&t.
Row 6 K18 B, w&t.
Row 8 K12 B, w&t.
Row 10 K6 B, w&t.

Gauge
24 sts and 44 rows to 4"/10cm over garter st using size 4 (3.5mm) needles.
Take time to check gauge.

Row 12 K36 B, break B, k6 A.
With A, knit 30 rows.

SHORT ROW WEDGE 2
Row 1 (RS) K6 A, change to B and k36.
Row 2 K6 B, w&t.
Row 3 and all odd-numbered rows Knit.
Row 4 K12 B, w&t.
Row 6 K18 B, w&t.
Row 8 K24 B, w&t.
Row 10 K30 B, w&t.
Row 12 Rep row 10.
Row 14 Rep row 8.
Row 16 Rep row 6.
Row 18 Rep row 4.
Row 20 Rep row 2.
Row 22 K36 B, cut B, k6 A.
With A, knit 30 rows.

SHORT ROW WEDGE 3
Work rows 1–11 as for wedge 2.
Row 12 K36 B, break B, k6 A.
With A, knit 30 rows.

SHORT ROW WEDGE 4
Work as for short row wedge 2.
With A, knit 30 rows.

SHORT ROW WEDGE 5
Work as for short row wedge 1.
With A, knit 30 rows.

SHORT ROW WEDGE 6
Work as for short row wedge 2.
With A, knit 30 rows.

SHORT ROW WEDGE 7
Work as for short row wedge 3.
With A, knit 30 rows. Bind off. This is the center left front edge.
Place markers (pm) along the top edge above the points of wedges 2, 4, and 6 to mark the side seam edges and the center back.

Yoke
With RS facing, circular needle and A, pick up and k 31 sts to the first marker, pm, pick up and k 32 sts to the center back marker, pm, pick up and k 32 sts to the 3rd marker, pm, K 31 sts to the left front edge—126 sts.
Working back and forth in rows, knit 10 rows.

DIVIDE FOR FRONTS AND BACK
Row 1 (WS) K28 and leave on hold for left front; bind off next 6 sts for underarm, k until there are 58 sts and leave on hold for back, bind off 6 sts for underarm and k to end. Cont on 28 sts for right front only.

SHAPE ARMHOLE
Next row (RS) Knit.
Next (dec) row (WS) K2tog, k to end—1 st dec'd.
Rep dec row every other row twice more—25 sts.
Knit 16 rows.

SHAPE NECK
Next row (RS) Bind off 7 sts, k to end.
Knit 1 row.
Next (dec) row (RS) K2tog, k to end—1 st dec'd.
Rep dec row every other row 5 times more—12 sts.
Knit 7 rows.

SHAPE SHOULDER
Row 1 (RS) K4, w&t.
Row 2 Knit.
Row 3 K8, w&t.
Row 4 Knit.
Row 5 K12, place sts on strand of scrap yarn.

LEFT FRONT
Rejoin A at armhole ready to work a RS row.
Next row (RS) Knit.
Next (dec) row (WS) K to last 2 sts, k2tog—1 st dec'd.
Rep dec row every other row twice more—25 sts.
Knit 17 rows.

SHAPE NECK
Next row (WS) Bind off 7 sts, k to end.
Next (dec) row (RS) K to last 2 sts, k2tog—1 st dec'd.
Rep dec row every other row 5 times more—12 sts.
Knit 8 rows.

SHAPE SHOULDER
Row 1 (WS) K4, w&t.
Row 2 Knit.
Row 3 K8, w&t.
Row 4 Knit.
Row 5 K12. Place sts on strand of scrap yarn.

BACK
Rejoin A, ready to work a RS row.
Next row (RS) Knit.
Next (dec) row (WS) K2tog, k to the last 2 sts, k2tog—2 sts dec'd.
Rep dec row every other row twice more—52 sts.
Work even until armhole measures 3½"/9cm.

Fancy Flared Jacket

SHAPE NECK
Next row (RS) K15, join a 2nd ball of yarn and bind off 22 sts, k to end. Working both sides at once, dec 1 st at each neck edge on the next 3 RS rows. Then, work the short row shoulder shaping as for front shoulders.

Pre-Finishing
Using the 3-needle bind-off method, join shoulders tog from the WS. Block piece very lightly to measurements.

Sleeves
With A, cast on 36 sts.
Knit 2 rows A, knit 2 rows B. Cont in garter st stripe pat, work as foll:
Next (inc) row (RS) Kfb, k to last 2 sts, kfb, k1—2 sts inc'd.
Rep inc row every alternate 6th and 4th row for 11 more inc rows—60 sts.
Work even until piece measures 6"/15cm from beg.

SHAPE CAP
Bind off 3 sts at beg of next 2 rows. Dec 1 st each side every other row 12 times, then dec 1 st each side every row 6 times—18 sts. Work 3 rows even. Bind off 3 sts at beg of next 2 rows. Bind off rem 12 sts.

RIB CUFF TRIM
With RS facing, *pick up and k 2 sts with A, 2 sts with B; rep from * 8 times more—36 sts. Cont in corrugated rib for 6 rows. Bind off knitwise with A using smaller needle. Block sleeves lightly. Set in sleeves. Sew sleeve seams.

NECKBAND
With RS facing and circular needle, pick up and k 2 sts with A, *2 sts with B, 2 sts with A; rep from * 23 times more—98 sts. Work the corrugated rib as for sleeve cuff.

BUTTON BAND
Working along the left front edge, pick up and k 2 sts with A, *2 sts with B, 2 sts with A; rep from * 15 times more—66 sts. Work the corrugated rib as for sleeve cuff.

BUTTONHOLE BAND
Pick up and k sts as for button band. Work 3 rows in corrugated rib.
Next (buttonhole) row (RS) [K2 A, p2 B] 3 times, k1 A, then bind off 3 sts, *[k2 A, p2 B] twice, k1 A, bind off 3 sts; rep from * 3 times more, k2 A.
Next row Work in corrugated rib, casting on 3 sts over each set of bound-off sts. Work 1 row even. Bind off with smaller needle. Sew on buttons to correspond to buttonholes. ■

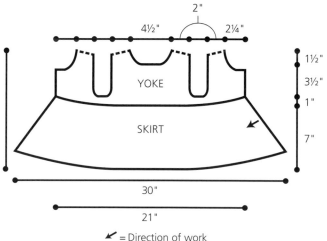

2"

4½"   2¼"

1½"

3½"

YOKE

1"

SKIRT

7"

30"

21"

↙ = Direction of work

39

Heather Striped V-Neck

One strand of a main color held together with four contrasting colors adds a soft, heathered look to a classic style.

DESIGNED BY CAROL J. SULCOSKI

Sizes
Instructions are written for size 3 months (6 months, 12 months). Shown in size 6 months.

Knitted Measurements
Chest 18 (20, 22½)"/45.5 (51, 57)cm
Length 8½ (9½, 10½)"/21.5 (24, 26.5)cm
Upper arm 8 (9, 10)"/20.5 (23, 25.5)cm

Materials
■ 2 1¾oz/50g skeins (each approx 180yd/165m) of Cascade Yarns *Cherub DK* (nylon/acrylic) in #41 blue mirage (MC)

■ 1 skein each in #47 teal (A), #36 cactus (B), #33 peacock (C), and #34 classic blue (D)

■ One each sizes 7 and 8 (4.5 and 5mm) circular needles, 16"/41cm long, *or size to obtain gauge*

■ One pair size 8 (5mm) needles

■ One set (5) each sizes 7 and 8 (4.5 and 5mm) double-pointed needles (dpns)

■ Stitch holder

■ Split ring stitch markers

K2, P1 Rib
(multiple of 3 sts)
Rnd 1 *K2, p1; rep from * to end.
Rep this rnd for k2, p1 rib.

Stripe Pattern 1
(for body)
Working in St st, *work 7 rnds MC/A held tog, 7 rnds MC/B held tog, 7 rnds MC/C held tog, 7 rnds MC/D held tog; rep from * (28 rnds) for stripe pat 1.

Stripe Pattern 2
(for sleeves)
Working in St st, *work 7 rnds MC/D held tog, 7 rnds MC/C held tog, 7 rnds MC/B held tog, 7 rnds MC/A held tog; rep from * (28 rnds) for stripe pat 2.

Notes
1) Use a double strand of yarn throughout.
2) Body is worked in the round to the underarms.
3) Sleeves are worked in the round.

Body
With smaller circular needle and 2 strands of MC held tog, cast on 81 (90, 102) sts. Join, being careful not to twist sts, and place marker (pm) for beg of rnds. Work around in k2, p1 rib for 1"/2.5cm, inc 1 (0, 0) st at end of last rnd— 82 (90, 102) sts. Change to larger circular needle, St st (k every rnd), and stripe pat 1 for body. Work even until piece measures 4½ (5, 5½)"/11.5 (12.5, 14)cm from beg.

DIVIDE FOR BACK AND FRONT
Change to straight needles.
Next row (RS) Work across first 41 (45, 51) sts; leave rem 41 (45, 51) sts on needle for front.

Gauge
18 sts and 26 rnds to 4"/10cm over St st using a double strand of yarn and larger circular needle. *Take time to check gauge.*

BACK

Work back and forth in St st (k on RS, p on WS) until armhole measures 4 (4½ 5)"/10 (11.5, 12.5)cm, end with a WS row.

SHOULDER AND NECK SHAPING

Next row (RS) Bind off first 10 (12, 14) sts for right back shoulder, k center 21 (21, 23) sts and place on st holder for back neck, bind off rem 10 (12, 14) sts for left back shoulder.

FRONT

Change to straight needles. Join 2 strands of color in progress. Work even in St st until armhole measures 1 (1½, 1½)"/2.5 (4, 4)cm, end with a WS row.

NECK SHAPING

Next row (RS) Work across first 19 (21, 24) sts, join another 2 strands of color in progress, SK2P over center 3 sts, place this st on holder, work across last 19 (21, 24) sts. Working both sides at once, bind off 2 sts from each neck edge 3 times, end with a WS row.

Dec row (RS) With first 2 strands of yarn, work to last 3 sts, k2tog, k1; with 2nd 2 strands of yarn, k1, ssk, work to end.

Next row Purl.

Rep last 2 rows 2 (2, 3) times more. Work even on 10 (12, 14) sts each side until piece measures same length as back to shoulder, end with a WS row. Bind off each side. Sew shoulder seams.

SLEEVES

With RS facing, dpns, and MC/A held tog, beg at underarm and pick up and k 38 (42, 46) sts evenly spaced around entire armhole edge. Divide sts evenly between 4 needles. Join and pm for beg of rnd. Work even in St st for 2 rnds. Cont in stripe pat 2 for sleeves. AT THE SAME TIME, shape sleeve as foll:

Dec rnd K2tog, knit to 2 sts before marker, ssk.

Next 3 rnds Knit. Rep these 4 rnds 5 (6, 7) times more. Work even on 26 (28, 30) sts until piece measures 4 (4½, 5)"/10 (11.5, 12.5)cm from beg, dec 2 (1, 0) sts evenly spaced across last rnd—24 (27, 30) sts. Change to smaller dpns and 2 strands of MC held tog. Work around in k2, p1 rib for 1"/2.5cm. Bind off loosely in rib.

Finishing

Lightly block piece to measurements.

NECKBAND

With RS facing, smaller circular needle, and 2 strands D held tog, pick up and k 21 (21, 24) sts evenly spaced along left front neck edge, k 1 st from holder then mark this st with split ring marker for center st, pick up and k 21 (21, 24) sts evenly spaced along right front neck edge, pick up and k 1 st in right shoulder seam, k 21 (21, 23) sts from back neck holder, inc 1 (1, 2) sts evenly spaced, then pick up and k 1 st in left shoulder seam—67 (67, 76) sts. Join and pm for beg of rnds.

Next rnd [P1, k2] 7 (7, 8) times, remove marker from center st, k1, mark this st again with split ring marker, [k2, p1] 15 (15, 17) times.

Dec rnd Work in rib to 1 st before marked st, remove marker, SK2P, then mark this st again with split ring marker, work in rib to end.

Next rnd Work even in rib as established. Rep last 2 rnds once more. Bind off loosely in rib. ■

2¼ (2½, 3)"

4½ (4½, 5)"   4 (4½, 5)" 1"

3 (3, 3½)"

5 (5¾, 6½)"

8 (9,10)"

5½ (6½, 7)"

FRONT & BACK

3½ (4, 4½)"

1"

18½ (20, 22½)"   ↑ = Direction of work

10

Anchors Aweigh Sweater

Set sail in this nautical knit with a graphic intarsia anchor
and accent stripes on the sleeves.

DESIGNED BY MATTHEW SCHRANK

■■■■

Sizes
Instructions are written for size 3 months
(6 months, 12 months, 18 months).
Shown in size 6 months.

Knitted Measurements
Chest 17 (18, 19, 20)"/43
(45.5, 48.5, 51)cm
Length 11 (12, 13, 14)"/28
(30.5, 33, 35.5)cm
Upper arm 7½ (8, 9, 10)"/19
(20.5, 23, 25.5)cm

Materials
■ 2 (2, 3, 3) 1¾oz/50g skeins (each
approx 180yd/165m) of Cascade Yarns
Cherub DK (nylon/acrylic) in #9 ecru (A)

■ 1 skein in #27 navy blue (B)

■ One pair size 5 (3.75mm) needles
or size to obtain gauge

■ One set (5) size 5 (3.75mm)
double-pointed needles (dpns)

■ Stitch markers

Stripe Pattern
In St st, work 2 rows A, 8 rows B, 6 rows
A, 8 rows B. These 24 rows comprise the
stripe pat.

Back
With A, cast on 58 (62, 68, 74) sts.
Next row (RS) K1, *k1, p1; rep
from * to last st, p1.
Next row K the knit sts and p the
purl sts for k1, p1 rib.
Cont in k1, p1 rib until piece measures
1½"/4cm from beg.

BEG SIDE SHAPING
Work in St st (k on RS, p on WS),
dec 1 st each side every 14th (16th, 18th,
18th) row 3 times, then every 4th (2nd,
2nd, 6th) row once—50 (54, 60, 66) sts.
Piece measures approx 7¼ (7¾, 8½,
9)"/18.5 (19.5, 21.5, 23)cm from beg,
end with a WS row. Place markers for
sleeves in each end of this row.
Work even in St st until piece measures
11 (12, 13, 14)"/ 28 (30.5, 33, 35.5)cm
from beg. Bind off.

Front
Work as for back, AT THE SAME TIME,
when rib is complete, work 0, 2, 6,
10 rows.

BEGIN CHART
Next row (RS) K14 (16, 19, 22),
place marker (pm), work row 1 of chart
over 30 sts, pm, k to end.
Cont as established, working side
shaping as for back, and foll chart until
row 31 of chart is complete. Work 0 (7,
11, 15) rows. Place markers to mark
center 8 sts.

SHAPE NECK
Next row (WS) P to marker, place
next 8 sts on a st holder, join 2nd ball of
A, p to end.
Working both sides at once with separate
balls of yarn, dec 1 st at each neck edge
every 4th row 10 (10, 11, 10) times, then
every other row 0 (0, 0, 2) times. When
all shaping is complete, work even on
rem 11 (13, 15, 17) shoulder sts each
side until piece measures same as back.
Bind off.

Sleeves
With A, cast on 30 (36, 40, 42) sts. Work
in k1, p1 rib as for back for 1½"/4cm,
end with a WS row.

Gauge
24 sts and 32 rows to 4"/10cm over St st using size 5 (3.75mm) needles. *Take time to check gauge.*

Anchors Aweigh Sweater

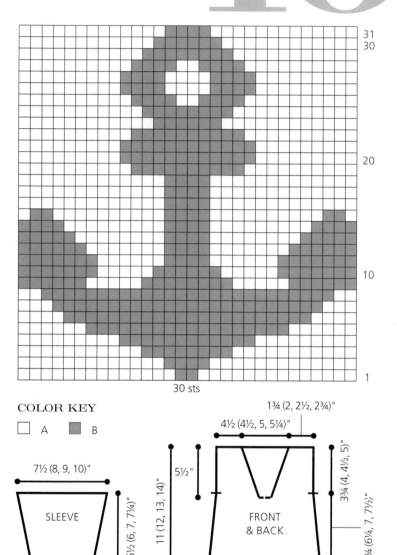

31
30
20
10
1

30 sts

COLOR KEY

☐ A ▨ B

SLEEVE

7½ (8, 9, 10)"
5½ (6, 7, 7¼)"
1½"
5 (6, 6½, 7)"

FRONT & BACK

1¾ (2, 2½, 2¾)"
4½ (4½, 5, 5¼)"
5½"
11 (12, 13, 14)"
3¾ (4, 4½, 5)"
5¾ (6¼, 7, 7½)"
1½"
9½ (10¼, 11¼, 12¼)"
8½ (9, 10, 11)"

BEG STRIPE PAT AND SLEEVE SHAPING

Work in stripe pat, AT THE SAME TIME, inc 1 st each side every 4th (6th, 6th, 4th) row 3 (4, 4, 1) times, then every 6th (8th, 8th, 6th) row 4 (2, 3, 8) times more—44 (48, 54, 60) sts. Work even in St st with A until sleeve measures 7 (7½, 8½, 8¾)"/18 (19, 21.5, 22)cm from beg. Bind off.

Finishing

Block pieces lightly to measurements. Sew shoulder seams. Center sleeves between markers and sew in place. Sew side and sleeve seams.

NECKBAND

Beg at right shoulder, with RS facing, dpns, and A, pick up and k 28 (28, 30, 32) sts along back neck, pick up and k 16 sts along left front neck, pm, k8 from front neck holder, pm, pick up and k 16 sts along right front neck, pm for beg of rnd—68 (68, 70, 72) sts.

Next rnd *K1, p1; rep from * to next marker, sl marker, SKP, p1, k1 to 2 sts before next marker, k2tog, sl marker, *p1, k1; rep from * to end.

Next rnd K the knit sts and p the purl sts to the next marker, sl marker, SKP, rib to 2 sts before next marker, k2tog, sl marker, rib to end.

Rep last rnd twice more. Bind off very loosely in rib. ■

Baby Shale Dress

This colorful dress with pretty shale lace at the sleeves, neck, and bottom can transition into a tunic sweater as baby grows.

DESIGNED BY HALLEH TEHRANIFAR

Sizes

Instructions are written for size 6 months (12 months). Shown in size 6 months.

Knitted Measurements

Chest 18 (20)"/45.5 (51)cm
Length 11 (12)"/28 (29)cm
Upper arm 6½ (7½)"/16.5 (19)cm

Materials

- 2 (3) 1¾oz/50g skeins (each approx 180yd/165m) of Cascade Yarns *Cherub DK* (nylon/acrylic) in #516 tiger lily
- One each sizes 3 and 5 (3.25 and 3.75mm) circular needle, 16"/40cm long, *or size to obtain gauge*
- One set (4) size 5 (3.75mm) double-pointed needles (dpns)
- Size F/5 (3.75mm) crochet hook
- Stitch markers, stitch holders
- One ⅝"/6mm button

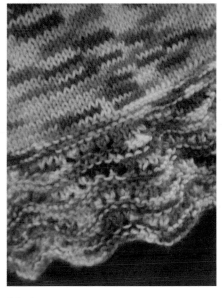

Note

Body and sleeves are worked flat over baby shale pat, then joined to work in St st in rnds. Sleeves and body are begun separately, then joined to work the yoke.

Baby Shale Pattern

(multiple of 11 sts plus 2)
Row 1 (RS) Knit.
Row 2 Knit.
Row 3 K1, *[k2tog] twice, [yo, k1] 3 times, yo, [skp] twice; rep from * to last st, k1.
Row 4 Purl.
Rows 5 and 6 Knit.
Rep rows 1–6 for baby shale pattern.

Sleeves

With larger circular needle, cast on 46 sts. Do not join.
Next row (WS) Knit.

BEG BABY SHALE PAT
Work rows 1–6 of baby shale pat 3 times.
For size 6 months only
Next (dec) row (RS) SKP, k5, k2tog, (k3, k2tog) 6 times, k5, k2tog—37 sts.
For size 12 months only
Next (dec) row (RS) SKP, k20, k2tog, 20, k2tog—43 sts.
For both sizes
Divide sts evenly on 3 dpns, join and place marker (pm) for beg of rnd.
Next rnd K1, *p1, k1; rep from * to end.
Rep last rnd 6 times more.
Next rnd Knit.
Work even in St st (knit every rnd) until sleeve measures 5 (5½)"/11.5 (12.5)cm from beg. Place last 6 sts and first 6 sts of rnd on holder for underarm, place rem

Gauges

23 sts and 32 rnds to 4"/10cm over St st using larger needle.
22 sts and 32 rows to 4"/10cm over baby shale pat using larger needle.
Take time to check gauges.

Baby Shale Dress

25 (31) sts on st holder for sleeve. Set sleeve aside.

Body
With larger circular needle, cast on (134, 145) sts. Do not join.
Next row (WS) Knit.
Work rows 1–6 of baby shale pat 4 times, dec 2 (1) sts evenly across last row—132 (144) sts.

DIVIDE FOR FRONT AND BACK
Next row (RS) K33 (36) for left back, pm for side, k66 (72) for front, pm for side, k33 (36) for right back, pm for beg of rnd. Knit 5 rnds.

SHAPE SIDES
Next (dec) rnd [Work to 3 sts before side marker, SKP, k1, sl marker, k1, k2tog]

twice, work to end of rnd—4 sts dec'd. Cont in St st and rep dec rnd every 6th (8th) rnd 3 times more, then every 4th rnd 3 times—104 (116) sts. Work even until piece measures 8 (8½)"/20.5 (21.5)cm from beg.

YOKE
Next rnd Work 20 (23) left back sts, pm for sleeve, sl next 12 sts to holder for underarm and remove side marker, work 25 (31) sleeve sts from holder, pm for sleeve, work 40 (46) front sts, sl next 12 sts to holder for underarm and remove side marker, pm for sleeve, work 25 (31) sleeve sts from holder, pm for sleeve, work 20 (23) right back sts—130 (154) sts. Knit 5 (6) rnds.

Next (dec) rnd [Work to 3 sts before sleeve marker, SKP, k1, sl marker, k1,

k2tog; rep from] 4 times, work to end of rnd—122 (146) sts. Cont in St st and rep dec rnd every other rnd 4 (7) times more—90 sts.

NECKBAND
Remove markers, turn and work back and forth in rows as foll:
Next row (WS) Knit.
Work rows 3–6 of baby shale pat. Change to smaller circular needle and rep rows 3–6 of baby shale pat once more.
Next (dec) row (RS) K1, *[k2tog] twice, k1, [yo, k1] twice, [SKP] twice; rep from * to last st, k1—74 sts.
Next row Purl.
Knit 2 rows. Bind off as foll: *p2tog, sl back to LH needle; rep from * to end. Do not break yarn.

Finishing
BUTTON LOOP
With crochet hook and working yarn, insert hook in last st on neckband and work sl st around back neck opening to first bound-off st of neckband, ch 8, join with sl st to last sl st to form button loop. Sew button to opposite corner of neckband.

Join underarm sts to sleeve sts using Kitchener st. Sew edges of lace borders closed on sleeves and body. Block gently to measurements. ■

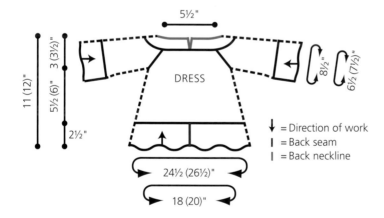

5½"

3 (3½)"

11 (12)"

5½ (6)"

2½"

DRESS

8½"

6½ (7½)"

↓ = Direction of work

I = Back seam

I = Back neckline

24½ (26½)"

18 (20)"

Sawtooth Edge Blanket

This bold garter stitch blanket is worked on the diagonal, with the sawtooth border knitted separately and sewn on.

DESIGNED BY KATHARINE HUNT

Knitted Measurements
Approx 26 x 32"/66 x 81cm

Materials
- 2 3½oz/100g skeins (each approx 240yd/220m) of Cascade Yarns *Cherub Aran* (nylon/acrylic) each in #14 melon (A), #09 ecru (B), and #11 key lime (C)
- One pair size 6 (4mm) needles *or size to obtain gauge*
- Size E/4 (3.5mm) crochet hook
- Safety pin
- Stitch holder

Stripe Sequence
In garter st, work *96 rows A, [12 rows B, 28 rows C] twice, 12 rows B. Rep from * until blanket is complete.

Blanket
With A, cast on 1 st. (K1, p1, k1) in cast-on st.
Next row Knit.

BEG STRIPE SEQUENCE
Next (inc) row (RS) (K1, p1) in first st, k to last st, (k1, p1) in last st—2 sts inc'd.
Working in garter st (k every row) and stripe sequence, rep inc row every other row until piece measures 26"/66cm along LH side, end with a WS row.
Next row (RS) (K1, p1) in first st, k to last 2 sts, k2tog.
Next row Knit.
Rep last 2 rows, working in stripe sequence as established, until piece measures 32"/81cm along RH side, end with a WS row.

Next (dec) row (RS) Ssk, k to last 2 sts, k2tog.
Cont in stripe sequence as established, and rep dec row every other row until 3 sts rem.
Next row SK2P. Fasten off.

Sawtooth Edging
With B, cast on 7 sts. Knit 2 rows.
Row 1 (RS) Yo, k2tog, yo, k to end— 1 st inc'd.
Rows 2, 6, and 8 Knit.
Rows 3, 5, 7, and 9 Rep row 1—12 sts.
Row 10 Bind off 5 sts, k to end—7 sts.
Rep rows 1–10 until border fits around entire edge of blanket, end with a row 9.
Next row Bind off 6 sts, k1, turn, k2, turn. Place sts on st holder.

Finishing
With B, crochet a round of slip st around entire edge of blanket. Sew edging to crochet round, easing edging around the corners. Adjust length of border if necessary. Bind off rem sts. Sew ends of border tog. ■

Gauge
20 sts and 40 rows to 4"/10cm over garter st using 6 (4mm) needles. *Take time to check gauge.*

Baseball Jacket

Make varsity with this eye-catching outer layer that sports pockets, a V-neck, and colorblock raglan sleeves.

DESIGNED BY CHERYL MURRAY

Sizes
Instructions are written for size 3 months (6 months, 12 months). Shown in size 6 months.

Knitted Measurements
Chest 18 (20, 22)"/45.5 (51, 56)cm
Length from shoulder 10 (11, 12)"/25.5 (28, 30.5)cm
Upper arm 7 (8, 8½)"/18 (20.5, 21.5)cm

Materials
■ 1 (2, 2) 1¾oz/50g skeins (each approx 180yd/165m) of Cascade Yarns *Cherub DK* (nylon/acrylic) in #27 navy blue (A)

■ 1 skein each in #9 white (B) and #51 gold (C)

■ One each sizes 3 and 4 (3.25 and 3.5mm) circular needle, 24"/60cm long, *or size to obtain gauge*

■ One set (5) each sizes 3 and 4 (3.25 and 3.5mm) double-pointed needles (dpns)

■ Five ⁹⁄₁₆"(13mm) buttons

■ Stitch markers, stitch holders

Garter Rib
(worked in rows)
(over an odd number of sts)
Row 1 (RS) Knit.
Row 2 *P1, k1; rep from * to end.
Rep rows 1 and 2 for garter rib worked in rows.

Garter Rib
(worked in rnds)
(over an even number of sts)
Rnd 1 Knit.
Rnd 2 *K1, p1; rep from * around.
Rep rnds 1 and 2 for garter rib worked in rnds.

Short Row Wrap and Turn (w&t)
on RS row (on WS row)
1) Wyib (wyif), sl next st purlwise.
2) Move yarn between the needles to the front (back).
3) Sl the same st back to LH needle. Turn work. One st is wrapped.
4) When working the wrapped st, insert RH needle under the wrap and work it tog with the corresponding st on needle to hide or close wrap.

Gauge
26 sts and 35 rows/rnds to 4"/10cm over St st using larger needles.
Take time to check gauge.

Baseball Jacket

Notes

1) Jacket is worked in one piece to the armholes. Sleeves are begun in the round and joined to the body to work the yoke with raglan shaping.

2) When changing colors, twist strands on WS to avoid holes in work.

Jacket

GARTER RIB

With smaller circular needle and A, cast on 109 (119, 129) sts. Do *not* join.

Rows 1 and 2 With A, work 2 rows in garter rib.

Row 3 With A, k7, join B and k to last 7 sts, join 2nd ball of A and k7.

Row 4 Cont in garter rib, work in colors as they appear.

Rows 5 and 6 Rep rows 1 and 2.

Row 7 (buttonhole RS) With A, k7; join C and k to last 7 sts, with 2nd ball of A, k2, yo, k2tog, k to end.

Rows 8–10 Cont in garter rib, work in colors as they appear.

Rows 11–14 Rep rows 1–4.

Row 15 Rep row 1.

Row 16 With A, work in garter rib over 7 sts, cont in garter rib to last 7 sts, inc 9 (13, 13) sts evenly across, work in garter rib over last 7 sts—118 (132, 142) sts. Break yarn. Place first and last 7 sts on st holders for front bands. Change to larger circular needle.

BODY

Next row (RS) Rejoin A, cast on 1 st, k23 (26, 28), place marker (pm) for side, k58 (66, 72), pm, k to end.

Next row (WS) Cast on 1 st, p to end, slipping markers—106 (120, 130) sts. Cont in St st until piece measures 5¾ (6½, 7)"/14.5 (16.5, 18)cm, end with a WS row. Place sts on st holder.

Sleeves

With smaller dpns and A, cast on 32 (36, 36) sts. Join, being careful not to twist sts, and pm for beg of rnd.

Work in garter rib in foll color sequence: 2 rnds A, 2 rnds B, 2 rnds A, 4 rnds C, 2 rnds A, 2 rnds B, 1 rnd A.

Next rnd With A, cont in garter rib, inc 4

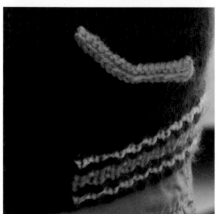

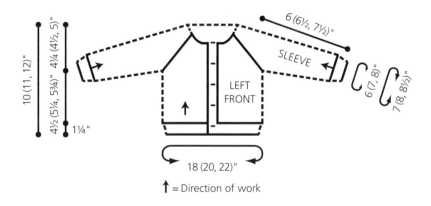

6 (6½, 7½)"

SLEEVE

LEFT FRONT

10 (11, 12)"

4½ (5¼, 5¾)" 4¼ (4½, 5)"

1¼"

6 (7, 8)"

7 (8, 8½)"

18 (20, 22)"

↑ = Direction of work

sts evenly around—36 (40, 40) sts.
Break yarn. Change to larger dpns.
Next (inc) rnd With B, k1, M1, k to last st, M1, k1—2 sts inc'd.
Work 5 (5, 3) rnds in St st (k every rnd).
Rep inc rnd every 6th rnd 3 (4, 7) times more, then every 8th rnd 1 (1, 0) time— 46 (52, 56) sts.
Work even in St st until sleeve measures 6 (6½, 7½)"/15 (16.5, 19)cm from beg.
Next rnd K to last 7 sts, place next 14 sts on a st holder, place rem 32 (38, 42) sts on a 2nd holder.
Make 2nd sleeve.

JOIN SLEEVES TO BODY

Next row (RS) With larger circular needle and A, work 17 (20, 22) body sts, place next 14 sts on holder for underarm, pm, with B, work 32 (38, 42) sts of first sleeve, pm, with 2nd ball of A, work 44 (52, 58) sts for back, pm, place next 14 sts on holder for underarm, pm, with 2nd ball of B, work 32 (38, 42) sts of 2nd sleeve, pm, with 3rd ball of A, k to end—142 (168, 186) sts.
Work even in St st for 1"/2.5cm, end with a WS row.

SHAPE RAGLAN AND NECK

Note Read before cont to knit; neck shaping begins before raglan shaping is complete.
Next (dec) row (RS) [Work to 2 sts before marker, ssk, sl marker, k2tog, sl marker] 4 times—8 sts dec'd.

Rep inc row every other row 9 (12, 14) times more—62 (64, 66) sts.
AT THE SAME TIME, when piece measures 9 (9½, 10)"/23 (24, 25.5)cm from beg, shape neck as foll: Bind off 2 sts at beg of next 4 rows, dec 1 st at each neck edge once.
When all shaping is complete, leave rem 52 (54, 56) sts on needle.

Finishing

RIGHT FRONT BAND

Place 7 sts of right front band from holder on smaller dpn, ready to work a RS row.
With A, work row 1 of garter rib.
Next row (WS) Cast on 1 st, work row 2 of garter rib.
Keeping st at inside edge in St st for selvage, work in garter rib until band measures same as front to beg of neck shaping, slightly stretched. Dec 1 st at end of last (WS) row. Place 7 sts on holder.

LEFT FRONT BAND

Place 7 sts from left band holder on smaller dpn.
With A, cast on 1 st and work in garter rib for 6 (10, 18) rows, keeping st at inside edge in St st for selvage.
Next (buttonhole) row (RS) K3, yo, k2tog, k to end.
Cont in garter rib with selvage st, rep buttonhole row every 20th row 3 times more. When band measures same as left front band, dec selvage st and place rem 7 sts on holder.

NECKBAND

Sew front bands to body.
With RS facing, smaller circular needle, and A, k 7 sts from right front band, pick up and k 8 sts along right front neck, k 52 (54, 56) sts from body holder, pick up and k 8 sts along left front neck, k 7 from left front band—82 (84, 86) sts.
Knit 1 (WS) row, dec 1 st at center back—81 (83, 85) sts.

BEGIN SHORT ROW SHAPING AND GARTER RIB

Next row (RS) Working in garter rib, [work to last 14 sts, pm, w&t] twice.
Next row (RS) With B, [work to next marker, remove marker, close wrap, k4, pm, w&t] twice.
Next row (RS) With A, [work to next marker, remove marker, close wrap, k4, pm, w&t] twice.
Next row (RS) With C, [work to next marker, remove marker, close wrap, k3, pm, w&t] twice.
Next row (RS) With A, [work to next marker, remove marker, close wrap, k3, pm, w&t] twice. Bind off loosely.

FAUX POCKETS (MAKE 2)

With smaller dpns and C, cast on 20 sts.
Bind off. Break yarn, leaving a long tail.
Using photo as guide for placement, with tail, sew to front of jacket.

Graft underarms. Sew buttons opposite buttonholes. ■

Preppy Vest

A simple center cable and color-tipped edges add flair
to an adorably jaunty sweater vest.

DESIGNED BY CAROL J. SULCOSKI

Sizes

Instructions are written for
size 3 months (6 months, 12 months).
Shown in size 3 months.

Knitted Measurements

Chest 18½ (21, 22½)"/47 (53.5, 57)cm
Length 9¾ (10¾, 13¼)"/25 (27.5, 33.5)cm

Materials

■ 1 3½oz/100g skein (each approx 240yd/220m) of Cascade Yarns *Cherub Aran* (nylon/acrylic) in #43 golden rod (MC)

■ 1 skein in #14 melon (CC)

■ One each sizes 7 and 8 (4.5 and 5mm) circular needles, 16"/40cm long, *or size to obtain gauge*

■ Cable needle (cn)

■ Stitch holders, stitch markers

Stitch Glossary

4-st RPC Sl 2 sts to cn and hold to *back*, k2, p2 from cn.
4-st LPC Sl 2 sts to cn and hold to *front*, p2, k2 from cn.

3-Needle Bind-Off

1) Hold right sides of pieces together on two needles. Insert 3rd needle knitwise into first st of each needle, and wrap yarn knitwise.
2) Knit these two sts together, and slip them off the needles. *Knit the next two sts together in the same manner.
3) Slip first st on 3rd needle over 2nd st and off needle. Rep from * in step 2 across row until all sts are bound off.

Vest

With smaller needle and MC, cast on 92 (104, 112) sts. Join, being careful not to twist sts, and place marker (pm) for beg of rnd. Break MC.
Next rnd With CC, *k2, p2; rep from * around for k2, p2 rib.
Work in rib as established for 1 (1½, 1½)"/2.5 (4, 4)cm.
Knit 1 rnd. Break CC.
Change to larger needle and MC.

BEGIN CHART

Next rnd K17 (20, 22), pm, work rnd 1 of chart over 12 sts, pm, k17 (20, 22), pm for side, k to end of rnd.
Cont to work in this way, slipping markers every rnd, until rnd 12 of chart is complete.
Rep rnds 1–12 for 1 (1, 2) times more, then rep rnds 1–6 once.

DIVIDE FOR FRONT AND BACK

Next rnd Work in pat to 4 sts before side marker, bind off 8 (10, 12) sts, removing marker, work to last 4 (5, 6) sts, bind off 8 (10, 12) sts, removing marker.
Working back and forth in rows on 38 (42, 44) sts for front, cont in pat until row 12 of chart is complete.

SHAPE NECK

Next row (RS) K to first marker, sl marker, p4, join a 2nd ball of yarn, ssk, k2tog, place last 2 sts on a stitch holder for front neck, p4, sl marker, k to end.
Working both sides at once with separate balls of yarn, bind off 2 sts from each neck edge twice, then 1 stitch from each neck edge once.
Work 1 row even.

Gauge

20 sts and 27 rnds to 4"/10cm over St st using larger needles. *Take time to check gauge.*

Preppy Vest

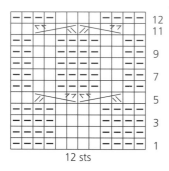

12 sts

STITCH KEY

☐ k on RS, p on WS

▭ p on RS, k on WS

4-st RPC

4-st LPC

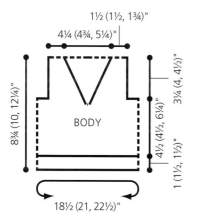

1½ (1½, 1¾)"

4¼ (4¾, 5¼)"

3¼ (4, 4½)"

8¾ (10, 12¼)"

4½ (4½, 6¼)"

BODY

1 (1½, 1½)"

18½ (21, 22½)"

Next (dec) row (RS) With first ball of yarn, work to last 4 sts, k2tog, k2; with 2nd ball of yarn, k2, ssk, k to end.
Rep dec row every other row 3 (4, 3) times more, then every 4th row 0 (1, 2) times.
Work even if necessary on 8 (8, 9) sts for each shoulder until armhole measures 3¼ (4, 4½)"/8 (10, 11.5)cm. Place sts on st holders.

BACK
Rejoin yarn to 38 (42, 44) back sts. Cont in St st until armholes measure same as front. Place center 22 (24, 26) sts on st holder for back neck.

Finishing
Carefully turn vest inside out and join shoulders using 3-needle bind-off method. Turn vest right side out.

NECKBAND
With smaller needle and MC, beg at right shoulder with RS facing, k 22 (24, 26) back neck sts, pick up and k 16 (17, 18) sts along left front neck, k2 from front neck holder, pm for center, pick up and k 16 (17, 18) sts along right front neck, pm for beg of rnd—56 (60, 64) sts.
Next rnd *K2, p2; rep from * around for k2, p2 ribbing.
Next (dec) rnd Rib to 1 st before marker, place new marker, S2KP, rib to end of rnd.
Next rnd Rib to marker, sl marker, k1, rib to end of rnd.
Rep dec rnd every other rnd twice more, keeping center st as a knit st. Work 1 rnd even. Break MC.
Join CC and bind off loosely in rib.

ARMHOLE TRIM
With smaller needle, CC, and RS facing, pick up and k 52 (56, 60) sts, pm.
Work in k2, p2 rib for 5 rnds. Break CC. Join MC and bind off loosely in rib. ■

Whale Yoke Pullover

You'll have a whale of a time knitting this top-down tunic-length sweater—and watching your little one wear it!

DESIGNED BY YELENA MALCOLM

Sizes

Instructions are written for size 3 months (6 months, 12 months). Shown in size 3 months.

Knitted Measurements

Chest 19½ (21½, 23½)"/49.5 (54.5, 59.5)cm
Length 11 (12, 13)"/28 (30.5, 33)cm

Materials

- 2 (3, 3) 1¾oz/50g skeins (each approx 180yd/165m) of Cascade Yarns *Cherub DK* (nylon/acrylic) in #33 peacock (A)

- 1 skein each in #5 baby mint (B) and #13 jade (C)

- Sizes 2 and 4 (2.75 and 3.5mm) circular needles, 20"/50cm long, *or size to obtain gauge*

- One set (4) size 4 (3.5mm) double-pointed needles (dpns)

- One set (5) size 2 (2.75mm) double-pointed needles

- Stitch holders, stitch markers

Note

Sweater is worked in the round from the neck down.

K1, P1 Rib

(over an even number of sts)
Rnd 1 *K1, p1; rep from * to end.
Rep rnd 1 for k1, p1 rib.

Sweater

YOKE
With smaller circular needle and A, cast on 108 (114, 120) sts. Place marker (pm) and join to work in the rnd, being careful not to twist sts. Work k1, p1 rib for 1"/2.5cm. Change to larger needle.

BEGIN SHAPING

Knit 0 (1, 1) rnd.
Next (inc) rnd Knit , inc 24 (25, 26) sts evenly around—132 (139, 146) sts.
Knit 1 rnd.
Next (inc) rnd Knit, inc 24 (25, 27) sts evenly around—156 (164, 173) sts. Break A. With B, knit 2 rnds.
Next (inc) rnd Knit, inc 24 (26, 27) sts evenly around—180 (190, 200) sts.
Knit 0 (0, 1) rnds.

BEGIN CHART

Join C and work chart as foll:
Rnd [Work 18-st rep, with B, k0 (1, 2)] 10 times around.
Cont to work chart in this manner until rnd 13 is complete.
Next (inc) rnd With B, knit, inc 18 (14, 19) sts evenly around—198 (204, 219) sts.
Knit 2 (1, 1) rnds.
Next (inc) rnd With B, knit, inc 0 (14, 19) sts evenly around—198 (218, 238) sts.
Knit 0 (1, 1) rnds. Break B and C.

Gauge

24 sts and 34 rnds to 4"/10cm over St st using larger needle. *Take time to check gauge.*

Whale Yoke Pullover

DIVIDE FOR ARMHOLES

With A, knit 0 (0, 2) rnds.

Next rnd Cast on 2 sts for underarm, K 55 (61, 67) sts for body, sl next 44 (48, 52) sts to holder for sleeve, cast on 4 sts for underarm, k 55 (61, 67) sts for body, sl next 44 (48, 52) sts to holder for sleeve, cast on 2 sts for underarm—118 (130, 142) body sts. Work in St st (k every rnd) until piece measures 10¼ (11¼, 12¼)"/26 (28.5, 31)cm from beg.

Change to smaller needle. Work in k1, p1 rib for ¾"/2cm. Bind off loosely in pat.

Sleeves

Place sts evenly on 4 dpns, pm for beg of rnd. Join A.

Next rnd Cast on 2 sts for underarm, k to end, cast on 2 sts for underarm—48 (52, 56) sts. Pm for beg of rnd. Work in St st for 1"/2.5cm.

Next (dec) rnd K1, k2tog, k to last 3 sts, ssk, k1—46 (50, 54) sts.

Rep dec rnd every 3rd (4th, 4th) rnd 7 times more—32 (36, 40) sts. Work even until sleeve measures 4½ (5, 5½)"/11.5 (12.5, 14)cm from underarm. Change to smaller dpns. Work in k1, p1 rib for ¾"/2cm. Bind off loosely in pat.

Finishing

Graft underarm sts on body to sleeve sts. Block lightly to measurements. ■

Color Key

☐ B

▨ C

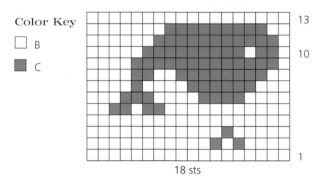

18 sts

13

10

1

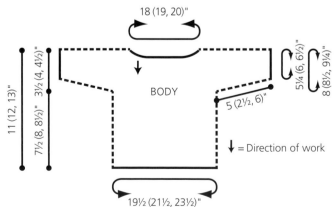

18 (19, 20)"

BODY

11 (12, 13)"

7½ (8, 8½)"

3½ (4, 4½)"

5¼ (6, 6½)"

8 (8½, 9¼)"

5 (2½, 6)"

↓ = Direction of work

19½ (21½, 23½)"

Cable & Slip Stitch Bunting

A textured stripe pattern covers a snuggly and sporty unisex bag with a front zipper for easy functionality.

DESIGNED BY KATHARINE HUNT

Sizes

Instructions are written for size 3–6 months (6–12 months). Shown in size 6–12 months.

Knitted Measurements

Chest 23 (28)"/58 (71)cm
Length 24 (25)"/61 (63.5)cm
Upper arm 9 (10)"/23 (25.5)cm

Materials

- 3 3½oz/100g skeins (each approx 240yd/220m) of Cascade Yarns *Cherub Aran* (nylon/acrylic) in #9 ecru (A)

- 2 skeins in #12 turquoise (B)

- One pair each sizes 5 and 6 (3.75 and 4mm) needles *or size to obtain gauge*

- Size 6 (4mm) circular needle, 24"/60cm long

- Size E/4 (3.5mm) crochet hook

- Cable needle (cn)

- Stitch holders, stitch markers

- One dress-weight zipper, 17"/43cm long

- Sewing needle and thread

Stitch Glossary

3-st RC Sl 2 sts to cn and hold to *back*, k1, k2 from cn.

Pattern Stitch (worked in rounds)

(multiple of 8 sts)
Rnd 1 With A, *3-st RC, k5; rep from * around.
Rnd 2 With A, knit.
Rnd 3 With B, *sl 3 wyib, [k1, sl 1 wyib] twice; rep from * around.
Rnd 4 With B, *sl 3 wyib, [p1, sl 1 wyif] twice; rep from * around.
Rep rnds 1–4 for pat st worked in rnds.

Pattern Stitch (worked in rows)

(multiple of 8 sts plus 5)
Row 1 (RS) With A, k5, *3-st RC, k5; rep from * to end.
Row 2 (WS) With A, purl.
Row 3 With B, [k1, sl 1 wyib] twice, k1, *sl 3 wyib, [k1, sl 1 wyib] twice, k1; rep from * to end.
Row 4 With B, [k1, sl 1 wyib] twice, k1, *sl 3 wyif, [k1, sl 1 wyib] twice, k1; rep from * to end.
Rep rows 1–4 for pat st in rows.

Bunting

With circular needle and A, cast on 144 (176) sts. Join, being careful not to twist sts, and place marker (pm) for beg of rnd.
Next rnd Work 3-st RC, pm, k5, work rnd 1 of pat st to end.
Cont in pat as established until piece measures 4½ (5)"/11 (12.5)cm from beg, end with a rnd 4.

DIVIDE FOR ZIPPER OPENING

Next rnd Bind off 3 sts, work rnd 1 of pat st to end of rnd—141 (173) sts. Turn, beg with row 2, work pat st in rows until piece measures 19½ (20)"/49.5 (51)cm from beg, end with a row 4.

SHAPE ARMHOLE

Next row (RS) Work next 34 (42) sts for right front, place these sts on a st holder, bind off 1 st, work in pat over next 71 (87) sts for back, place rem sts for left front on a st holder.
Cont in pat as established over 71 (87) back sts only, working first and last sts of rows 3 and 4 as k1, until armhole measures 4½ (5)"/11 (12.5)cm, end with a row 1. With A, bind off.

Gauge

25 sts and 42 rnds to 4"/10cm over pat st using size 6 (4mm) needle.
Take time to check gauge.

Cable & Slip Stitch Bunting

46

RIGHT FRONT
Place 34 (42) sts on needle, ready to work a WS row.
Beg at armhole edge, cont in pat as established for 2½ (3)"/6.5 (7.5)cm, end with a row 4.

SHAPE NECK
Bind off 8 sts at beg of next row. Dec 1 st at neck edge every other row 8 times. Work even in pat on rem 18 (26) sts until armhole measures same as back, end with a row 1. With A, bind off.

LEFT FRONT
Place 35 (43) sts for left front on needle, ready to work a RS row.
Bind off 1 st, cont in pat as established to end of row.
Cont in pat as established for 2½ (3)"/6.5 (7.5)cm, end with a row 1.

SHAPE NECK
Bind off 8 sts at beg of next row. Dec 1 st at neck edge every other row 8 times. Work even in pat on rem 18 (26) sts until armhole measures same as back, end with a row 1. With A, bind off.

Sleeves
With smaller straight needles and A, cast on 39 sts.
Next row (RS) [K1, p1] 3 times, *3-st RC, [p1, k1] twice, p1; rep from *, end last rep k1.
Next row K the knit sts and p the purl sts.
Rep last 2 rows 4 times more. Change to larger straight needles.

BEG PAT STITCH
Next row (RS) K1, work row 1 of pat st to last st, k1.

Next row (WS) K1, work row 2 of pat st to last st, k1.
Cont in pat st as established, inc 1 st each side every pat row 3, working inc'd sts into pat 10 (15) times—59 (65) sts. Work even until sleeve measures 6 (6½)"/15 (16.5)cm from beg, end with a row 1.
With A, bind off.

Finishing
Sew shoulder seams.

NECK TRIM
With RS facing. smaller needles, and A, pick up and k 29 sts along right front neck edge, pick up and k 32 sts along back neck, pick up and k 29 sts along left front neck edge—93 sts.
Next row (WS) *[K1, p1] twice, k1, p3; rep from * to last 5 sts, [k1, p1] twice, k1.
Next row (RS) *[P1, k1] twice, p1, 3-st RC; rep from * to last 5 sts, [p1, k1] twice, p1. Rep these 2 rows twice more. Bind off in pat.

ZIPPER OPENING
With crochet hook and A, beg at top of left front neck band, work a row of slip st into the center of each edge st along the entire zipper opening. Break yarn. Rejoin yarn to top of left front neck, work a row of slip st into the first row of slip st.

Sew zipper in place. Sew sleeves into armholes. Sew sleeve seams. Making sure that patterns are aligned and sides are even, sew cast-on edge tog. ∎

5¼" 3 (4¼)"

4½ (5)"

BODY

24 (25)"

15"

4½ (5)"

23 (28)"

9½ (10½)"

SLEEVE

5 (5½)"

1"

6¼"

Striped Raglan Cardigan

This simple cardi sports baseball-inspired style, thanks to multicolor stripes on the body and solid raglan sleeves.

DESIGNED BY SANDI PROSSER

Sizes
Instructions are written for size 3 months (6 months, 12 months). Shown in size 6 months.

Knitted Measurements
Chest (closed) 18 (20, 22)"/45.5 (51, 56)cm
Length 9½ (10½, 11½)"/24 (26.5, 29)cm
Upper arm 7½ (8½, 9½)"/19 (21.5, 24)cm

Materials
■ 2 1¾oz/50g skeins (each approx 180yd/165m) of Cascade Yarns *Cherub DK* (nylon/acrylic) in #8 baby blue (MC)

■ 1 skein each in #21 grass (A), #27 navy (B), and #42 apple cinnamon (C)

■ One pair each sizes 3 and 4 (3.25 and 3.5mm) needles *or size to obtain gauge*

■ Stitch holders

■ Five ½"/13mm buttons

K2, P2 Rib
(multiple of 4 sts plus 2)
Row 1 (RS) K2, *p2, k2; rep from * to end.
Row 2 K the knit sts and p the purl sts.
Rep row 2 for k2, p2 rib.

Stripe Pattern
Working in St st, *work 8 rows A, 4 rows MC, 4 rows B, 8 rows C, 4 rows MC, 4 rows B; rep from * (32 rows) for stripe pat.

Back
With smaller needles and MC, cast on 66 (70, 78) sts. Work in k2, p2 rib for 8 rows, dec 4 (2, 2) sts evenly spaced across last row, end with WS row—62 (68, 76) sts. Change to larger needles, St st, and stripe pat. Work even until piece measures 5 (5½, 6)"/12.5 (14, 15)cm from beg, end with a WS row.

RAGLAN SHAPING
Bind off 3 (3, 4) sts at beg of next 2 rows.
Row 1 (dec RS) K1, k2tog, knit to last 3 sts, SKP, k1.
Row 2 (dec) K1, p2tog tbl, purl to last 3 sts, p2tog, k1.
Row 3 (dec) K1, k2tog, knit to last 3 sts, SKP, k1.
Row 4 K1, p to last st, k1. Rep rows 3 and 4 for 14 (16, 18) times more. Place 22 (24, 26) sts on holder for back neck.

Left Front
With smaller needles and MC, cast on 30 (34, 38) sts. Work k2, p2 rib for 8 rows, dec 1 (2, 2) sts across last row, end with WS row—29 (32, 36) sts. Change to larger needles, St st, and stripe pat. Work even until piece measures same as back to underarms, end with WS row.

RAGLAN AND NECK SHAPING
Next row (RS) Bind off first 3 (3, 4) sts. Work next row even.
Row 1 (dec RS) K1, k2tog, knit to end.
Row 2 (dec) Purl to last 3 sts, p2tog, k1.
Row 3 (dec) K1, k2tog, knit to end.
Row 4 Purl to last st, k1. Rep rows 3 and 4 for 10 (12, 14) times more, then row 3 once—12 (13, 14) sts. Cont raglan shaping and beg neck shaping as foll:

Gauge
27 sts and 36 rows to 4"/10cm over St st using larger needles. *Take time to check gauge.*

47

Striped Raglan Cardigan

Next row (WS) Bind off first 3 (4, 5) sts, purl to last st, k1—9 sts.
Row 1 (dec RS) K1, k2tog, k3, SKP, k1—7 sts.
Row 2 (dec) K1, p2tog tbl, p3, k1—6 sts.
Row 3 (dec) K1, k2tog, SKP, k1—4 sts.
Row 4 K1, p2, k1.
Row 5 (dec) K1, k2tog, k1—3 sts.
Row 6 K1, p1, k1.
Row 7 (dec) K1, k2tog—2 sts.
Row 8 P1, k1.
Row 9 K2tog. Fasten off last st.

Right Front

Work as for left front until piece measures same as back to underarms, end with a RS row.

RAGLAN AND NECK SHAPING

Next row (WS) Bind off first 3 (3, 4) sts.
Row 1 (dec) Knit to last 3 sts, SKP, k1.
Row 2 (dec) K1, p2tog tbl, purl to end.
Row 3 (dec) Knit to last 3 sts, SKP, k1.
Row 4 K1, purl to end.
Rep rows 3 and 4 for 11 (13, 15) times more—12 (13, 14) sts. Cont raglan shaping and beg neck shaping as foll:
Row 1 (dec RS) Bind off first 3 (4, 5) sts, knit to last 3 sts, SKP, k1—8 sts.
Row 2 (dec) K1, p4, p2tog, k1—7 sts.
Row 3 (dec) K1, k2tog, k1, SKP, k1—5 sts.
Row 4 (dec) K1, p1, p2tog, k1—4 sts.
Row 5 (dec) K1, SKP, k1—3 sts.
Row 6 K1, p1, k1.

Row 7 (dec) SKP, k1—2 sts.
Row 8 K1, p1.
Row 9 K2tog. Fasten off last st.

Sleeves

With smaller needles and MC, cast on 42 (42, 46) sts. Work k2, p2 rib for 10 rows, dec (inc, inc) 1 st in center of last row, end with a WS row—41 (43, 47) sts. Change to larger needles and St st. Work 4 rows even, end with WS row.
Inc row (RS) K1, M1, knit to last st, M1, k1—2 sts inc'd.
Rep inc row every 8th (6th, 6th) row 4 (6, 7) times more. Work even on 51 (57, 63) sts until piece measures 6 (6½, 7)"/15 (16.5, 18)cm, end with WS row.

RAGLAN SHAPING

Bind off 3 (3, 4) sts at beg of next 2 rows—45 (51, 55) sts. Work even for 4 (2, 4) rows.
Row 1 (dec RS) K1, k2tog, knit to last 3 sts, SKP, k1—2 sts dec'd.
Row 2 K1, purl to last st, k1. Rep these 2 rows 13 (16, 17) times more. Place rem 17 (17, 19) sts on holder.

Finishing

Lightly block pieces. Sew armholes.

NECKBAND

With RS facing, smaller needles, and MC, pick up and k 8 (9, 10) sts evenly along

right front neck edge, k 17 (17, 19) sts from right sleeve holder, 22 (24, 26) sts from back neck holder, 17 (17, 19) sts from left sleeve holder, pick up and k 8 (9, 10) sts evenly along left front neck edge—72 (76, 84) sts.
Row 1 (WS) K1, *p2, k2; rep from *, end p2, k1.
Row 2 (WS) P1, *k2, p2; rep from *, end k1, p1. Rep rows 1 and 2 twice more. Bind off loosely in rib.

BUTTON BAND

With RS facing, smaller needles, and MC, pick up and k 66 (74, 82) sts evenly along right front edge. Beg with row 2, work k2, p2 rib for 6 rows, end with a WS row. Bind off loosely in rib.

BUTTONHOLE BAND

With RS facing, smaller needles, and MC, pick up and k 66 (74, 82) sts evenly along left front edge. Beg with row 2, work in k2, p2 rib for 2 rows, end with a RS row.
Next (buttonhole) row (WS) Rib first 4 sts, *p2tog, yo, rib next 12 (14, 16) sts; rep from * 3 times more, end p2tog, yo, rib to end. Rib 3 rows more. Bind off in rib. Sew side, sleeve seams. Sew on buttons. ■

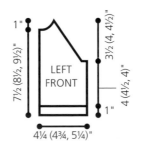

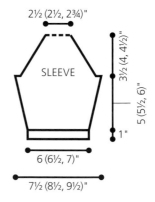

48

Circular Coverall

Uniquely lovely and uniquely useful, this medallion with sleeves will fit for a long time and serve as a perfect nursing coverup.

DESIGNED BY CHERI ESPER

Sizes
Instructions are written for size newborn–3 months (3–6 months). Shown in size 3–6 months.

Knitted Measurements
Circumference 29"/73cm

Materials
■ 5 (6) 1¾oz/50g skeins (each approx 180yd/165m) of Cascade Yarns *Cherub DK Multis* (nylon/acrylic) in #512 lily pond

■ One set (5) size 5 (3.75mm) double-pointed needles (dpns) *or size to obtain gauge*

■ Two size 5 (3.75mm) circular needles, 24 and 40"/60 and 100cm long

■ Stitch markers

Stitch Glossary
pfb Purl into the front and back of the next st to inc 1 st.

Coverall
Note Change to circular needle and longer circular needle as needed.
Cast on 9 sts. Divide on 4 dpns. Join, being careful not to twist sts, and place marker (pm) for beg of rnd.

SET-UP RNDS
Set-up rnd 1 Purl.
Set-up rnd 2 [P2, pfb] 3 times around—12 sts.
Set-up rnd 3 Knit.
Set-up rnd 4 [K4, M1] 3 times around—15 sts.
Set-up rnd 5 [P3, pm] 5 times around.

BEG INNER PAT
Rnd 1 (inc) [P to 1 st before marker, pfb, sl marker] 5 times around—5 sts inc'd.
Rnd 2 Knit.
Rnd 3 (inc) [K to marker, M1, sl marker] 5 times around—5 sts inc'd.
Rnd 4 Purl.

Rep rnds 1–4 for 9 (11) times more for inner pat, then rep rnds 1 and 2 once—120 (140) sts.

SHAPE ARMHOLE
Next rnd K17 (25), bind off 20 (22) sts, k until there are 46 sts on needle after bind-off, bind off 20 (22) sts, k to end of rnd.
Next rnd Knit, casting on 20 (20) sts over bound-off sts.
Next rnd Purl.
Cont to rep rows 1–4 of inner pat for 8 (6) times more—200 sts.
Next rnd [P20, pm, p20, sl marker] 5 times around.

BEG OUTER PAT
Rnd 1 (inc) [P to 1 st before marker, pfb, sl marker] 10 times around—10 sts inc'd.
Rnd 2 Knit.
Rnd 3 (inc) [K to marker, M1, sl marker] 10 times around—10 sts inc'd.
Rnd 4 Purl.
Rep rnds 1–4 for outer pat until piece measures 29"/73cm in diameter. Bind off.

SLEEVES
With dpns, pick up and k 42 (46) sts around armhole opening, pm for beg of rnd. Knit 2 rnds, purl 2 rnds until sleeve measures 7 (8)"/18 (20.5)cm from beg, or desired length. Bind off loosely. ■

Gauge
22 sts and 26 rows to 4"/10cm over St st using size 5 (3.75mm) needles. *Take time to check gauge.*

❋ Pattern for Textured
Leg Warmers is on page 60.

Ruffled Jumper

A garment for all seasons, this easy-knit jumper features handy buttoned shoulders and seed stitch texture.

DESIGNED BY MARGRET WILLSON

Sizes
Instructions are written for size 3 months (6 months, 12 months). Shown in size 6 months.

Knitted Measurements
Chest 17¼ (18½, 20)"/44 (47, 51)cm
Length 13½ (14½, 15½)"/34.5 (37, 39.5)cm

Materials
- 2 (2, 3) 1¾oz/50g skeins (each approx 180yd/165m) of Cascade Yarns *Cherub DK* (nylon/acrylic) in #37 lime sherbet
- One pair size 4 (3.5mm) needles *or size to obtain gauge*
- Size 4 (3.5mm) circular needle, 21"/53cm long
- Two ⅝"/15mm buttons

Seed Stitch
(over an even number of sts)
Row 1 *K1, p1; rep from * to end.
Row 2 P the knit sts and k the purl sts.
Rep row 2 for seed st.

Dress
SKIRT
With circular needle, cast on 152 (168, 184) sts. Join, being careful not to twist sts, and place marker (pm) for beg of rnd.

BEGIN CHART
Rnd 1 Work 8-st rep 19 (21, 23) times around.
Cont to follow chart in this manner until rnd 18 is complete. Work even in St st (knit every rnd) until skirt measures 8½ (9, 9½)"/21.5 (23, 24)cm from beg.
Next (dec) rnd Knit around, decreasing 48 (56, 64) sts evenly spaced—104 (112, 120) sts.

BEGIN CHART
Rnd 1 Work 8-st rep 13 (14, 15) times around. Cont to follow chart until rnd 17 has been worked.
Rnd 18 Work 52 (56, 60) sts for back, pm for side, work 52 (56, 60) sts for front.

Continue in rows of seed st as established for rest of project.

DIVIDE FOR FRONT AND BACK
Next row (RS) With straight needle, bind off 3 sts, work to marker—49 (53, 57) sts. Turn work, leave rem sts for front on circular needle to work later.
Next row Bind off 3 sts, work to end—46 (50, 54) sts.
Working back and forth in rows of seed st, cont to dec 1 st each side every other row 2 (2, 3) times—42 (46, 48) sts. Work even in seed st until armhole measures 3 (3½, 4)"/7.5 (9, 10)cm, end with a WS row.

BUTTON TABS
Next row (RS) Work across 11 sts for button tab, join 2nd ball of yarn and bind off 20 (24, 26) sts for back neck, work to end for button tab. Working both sides at once with separate balls of yarn, cont in seed st for 5 more rows.
Next (buttonhole) row (RS) [Work 4 sts, bind off 3 sts for buttonhole, work to end] over each tab.

Gauge
24 sts and 32 rnds to 4"/10cm over St st using size 4 (3.5mm) needles.
Take time to check gauge.

Ruffled Jumper

Next row Work across each tab, casting on 3 sts over bound-off sts.
Work even for 3 rows—armhole measures approx 4½ (5, 5½)"/11.5 (12.5, 14)cm. Bind off in pat.

FRONT
Join yarn to front sts for RS row.
Work as for back until armhole measures 1½ (1¾, 2)"/4 (4, 5)cm, end with a WS row.
Next row (RS) Work across 14 sts for shoulder, join 2nd ball of yarn and bind off 14 (18, 20) sts for front neck, work to end for shoulder. Work both sides at once, dec 1 st at neck edge every RS row 3 times more—11 sts rem each side.
Work even until armhole measures 3 (3½, 4)"/7.5 (9, 10)cm.
Bind off in pat.

Finishing
Block lightly to measurements. Sew buttons to shoulder fronts opposite buttonholes. ∎

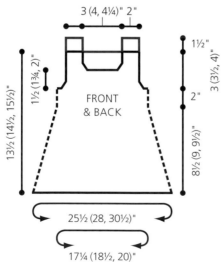

3 (4, 4¼)" 2"

1½"

1½ (1¾, 2)"

3 (3½, 4)"

FRONT & BACK

13½ (14½, 15½)"

2"

8½ (9, 9½)"

25½ (28, 30½)"

17¼ (18½, 20)"

▌ = Back neckline and buttonhole flap

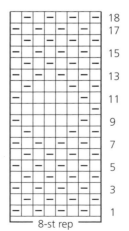

18
17
15
13
11
9
7
5
3
1

8-st rep

Stitch Key

☐ k on RS, p on WS

⊟ p on RS, k on WS

Lace Cardi & Bonnet

A perfect match for a perfect girl: this delicate all-seasons set features an open-front cardi and a bonnet tied with a ribbon.

DESIGNED BY DIANE ZANGL

Materials
- 3 1¾oz/50g skeins (each approx 180yd/165m) of Cascade Yarns *Cherub DK* (nylon/acrylic) in #32 cotton candy
- Size 6 (4mm) circular needle, 24"/60cm long, *or size to obtain gauge*
- One set (4) size 6 (4mm) double-pointed needles (dpns)
- Size G/6 (4.5mm) crochet hook
- Stitch holders, stitch markers
- Three 7/16"/11.5mm ball buttons
- ⅔yd/.75m of ¼" satin ribbon

Lace Pattern
(multiple of 6 sts plus 3)
Row 1 (RS) K3, *yo, S2KP, yo, k3; rep from * to end.
Rows 2 and 4 Purl.
Row 3 Yo, S2KP, yo, *k3, yo, S2KP, yo; rep from * to end.
Rep rows 1–4 for lace pat.

Body
With circular needle, loosely cast on 117 (129) sts.
Row 1 (WS) Sl 1, k to end.
Rows 2–7 Rep row 1.

BEG LACE PAT ST
Row 1 (RS) Sl 1, k5, place marker (pm), work lace pat over next 105 (117) sts, pm, k6.

Gauges
19 sts and 32 rows/rnds to 4"/10cm over lace pat using size 6 (4mm) needles.
22 sts and 32 rows/rnds to 4"/10cm over St st using size 6 (4mm) needles.
Take time to check gauges.

Lace Cardi & Bonnet

Row 2 (WS) Sl 1, k5, p to last 6 sts, k6. Keeping first and last 6 sts of every row in garter st with a sl st edge, cont to work the 4-row lace pat until piece measures 6½ (7¼)"/16.5 (18.5)cm from beg, end with a WS row. On the last WS row, pm at 29 (32) sts for left front, 59 (65) sts for back, and 29 (32) sts for right front.

SEPARATE AT ARMHOLE

Next row (RS) Sl 1, k to 8 sts before first marker, bind off next 16 sts, k to 8 sts before next marker, bind off 8 sts and turn, leaving rem sts on hold for left front.

BACK

Working the 43 (49) back sts only, beg with a WS row, knit 3 rows more (for garter ridge). Then, beg with a k row, cont in St st for 3 (3¼)"/7.5 (9.5)cm. Place markers to mark the center 11 (13) sts on the last WS row.

SHAPE NECK

Next row (RS) K to marked sts, join a 2nd ball of yarn and bind off 11 (13) sts, k to end. Working both sides at once, dec 1 st at each neck edge on every row 3 times. Bind off rem 13 (15) sts each side for shoulders.

LEFT FRONT

Rejoin yarn at armhole from the RS to work left front and bind off 8 sts, k to end—21 (24) sts. Cont to work 6 center edge sts in garter st with a sl st edge and rem sts in St st, work even until armhole measures 2½ (3¼)"/6.5 (8)cm.

SHAPE NECK

Next row (RS) K to last 6 sts, sl these 6 sts to a st holder, turn. Work 1 row even.
Dec row (RS) K to last 3 sts, k2tog, k1—1 st dec'd.
Rep dec row every other row 1 (2) times more—13 (15) sts. Work even until armhole measures same as back. Bind off sts for shoulder.

RIGHT FRONT

Rejoin yarn at armhole to work next row on WS on the 21 (24) sts and p to last 6 sts, k6.
Buttonhole row (RS) Sl 1, k2, yo, k2tog, k to end of row.
Cont as for left front, rep buttonhole row every 10th row (12th) row once more. Work even until armhole measures 2½ (3¼)"/6.5 (8)cm.

SHAPE NECK

Next row (RS) K6 and sl these sts to a holder, k1, SKP, k to end—1 st dec'd. Cont to dec 1 st at neck edge every RS row 1 (2) times more—13 (15) sts. Work even until armhole measures same as back. Bind off sts for shoulder.

Sleeves

With circular needle, loosely cast on 28 (32) sts. Knit 7 rows. Then, cont in St st, inc 1 st each side every 6th row 5 (7) times—38 (46) sts. Work even until piece measures 6½ (7½)"/16.5 (19)cm from beg. Pm each side of row. Work even for 1¼"/3cm from the markers (to fit into armhole bind-offs). Bind off.

Finishing

Sew shoulder seams. Set sleeves into armholes. Sew sleeve seams.

NECKBAND

With circular needle, from the RS, sl 1, then k 5 sts from holder, pick up and k 36 (40) sts around neck edge, k 6 sts from holder—48 (52) sts. Keeping the sl st edge at beg of every row, k 3 rows.
Buttonhole row (RS) Sl 1, k2, yo, k2tog, k to end. K 3 rows more. Bind off. Sew on buttons.

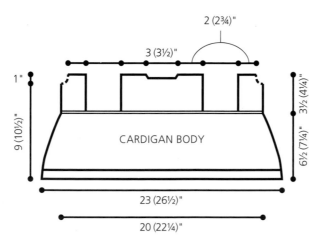

7 (8½)"
1¼"
SLEEVE
6½ (7½)"
5 (6)"
— = Marker

2 (2¾)"
3 (3½)"
1"
9 (10½)"
CARDIGAN BODY
6½ (7½)"
3½ (4¼)"
23 (26½)"
20 (22¼)"

Lace Cardi & Bonnet

Bonnet

Note Bonnet is worked in rnds for the circular crown at the back and then worked straight for the face edge. With dpns, cast on 6 sts, dividing sts evenly on 3 dpns. Join, being careful not to twist sts, and pm for beg of rnd.
Rnd 1 [K1, M1] twice on each needle—12 sts.

Rnd 2 and all even-numbered rnds Knit.
Rnd 3 [K2, yo] twice on each needle—18 sts.
Rnd 5 [K3, yo] twice on each needle—24 sts.
Rnd 7 [K4, yo] twice on each needle—30 sts.
Odd-numbered rnds 9–19 Cont to inc on each consecutive rnd by [k 1 more st than previous rnd, yo] twice on each needle—66 sts on rnd 19. Knit 1 rnd.

SIDES
Change to circular needle. With circular needle, bind off 11 sts (for back neck edge), purl to end of row—55 sts. At this point, work back and forth in rows.
Next row (WS) Purl, inc 2 sts evenly across—57 sts.

BEG LACE PAT
Row 1 (RS) Sl 1, k2, work lace pat over next 51 sts, k3.
Row 2 (WS) Sl 1, k2, p to last 3 sts, k3.
Keeping first and last 3 sts of every row in garter st with a sl st edge, cont in the 4-row lace pat until lace portion measures 3½"/9cm, end with a WS row. Knit 4 rows.
Eyelet row (RS) Sl 1, k1, *yo, k2tog; rep from *, end k1.
Knit 3 more rows. Bind off. With crochet hook, work an edge of single crochet from the RS in the 11 sts at the back neck edge. Thread the ribbon through the eyelet row and trim to desired length. ■

51

Colorblock Cabled Pullover

Sporty blocks of color put a fresh twist on a traditional Aran crewneck with handy shoulder buttons.

DESIGNED BY HOLLI YEOH

■■■▢

Sizes
Instructions are written for size 3 months (6 months, 12 months). Shown in size 6 months.

Knitted Measurements
Chest 19 (21½, 23½)"/48 (55.5, 59.5)cm
Length 10½ (11½, 12½)"/26.5 (29, 31.5)cm
Upper arm 8 (9, 10)"/20.5 (23, 25.5)cm

Materials
■ 2 3½oz/100g skeins (each approx 240yd/220m) of Cascade Yarns *Cherub Aran* (nylon/acrylic) in #21 grass (A)

■ 1 (1, 2) skeins in #47 teal (B)

■ One pair each sizes 6 and 7 (4 and 4.5mm) needles *or size to obtain gauge*

■ One spare size 7 (4.5mm) needle for 3-needle bind-off

■ Cable needle (cn)

■ Stitch holders

■ Three ⅝"/16mm buttons

Stitch Glossary
4-st LC Sl 2 sts to cn and hold to *front*, k2, k2 from cn.

Back
With smaller needles and A, cast on 58 (65, 71) sts.

BEG CHART PAT
Row 1 (RS) Beg with st 1 (5, 2) and work to rep line, work 15-st rep 2 (3, 3) times across, then work to st 43 (39, 42). Cont to foll chart in this way through row 12,

then rep rows 1–12 for pat. AT THE SAME TIME, when piece measures 1"/2.5cm from beg, change to larger needles. Work even until piece measures approx 5½ (6, 6½)"/14 (15, 16.5)cm from beg, end with a row 2 or 8. Change to B.
Next row (RS) Knit.
Beg with row 4 or 10, cont in chart pat and work even until piece measures 6½ (7, 7½)"/16.5 (18, 19)cm from beg, end with a WS row.

ARMHOLE SHAPING
Bind off 4 (5, 6) sts at beg of next 2 rows. Work even on 50 (55, 59) sts until armhole measures 4 (4½, 5)"/10 (11.5, 12.5)cm, end with a WS row.

SHOULDER AND NECK SHAPING
Next row (RS) Work across first 12 (14, 16) sts, place these sts on holder for right back shoulder, bind off center 26 (27, 27) sts for back neck, work across rem 12 (14, 16) sts for button band. Turn.

BUTTON BAND
Change to smaller needles.
Next row (WS) *K1, p1; rep from * to end. Rep this row 4 times more. Bind off loosely in rib.

Gauge
24 sts and 32 rows to 4"/10cm over chart pat using larger needles (slightly stretched). *Take time to check gauge.*

Colorblock Cabled Pullover

Front

Work as for back until armhole measures 2 (2½, 3)"/5 (6.5, 7.5)cm, end with a WS row.

NECK SHAPING

Next row (RS) Work across first 19 (21, 23) sts, join a 2nd ball of B and bind off center 12 (13, 13) sts, work to end. Working both sides at once, bind off from each neck edge 3 sts once, 2 sts once, then 1 st twice. Work even on 12 (14, 16) sts each side until piece measures same length as back to shoulder, end with a WS row.

SHOULDER SHAPING

Next row (RS) Work across first 12 (14, 16) sts for left front buttonhole band; with 2nd ball of yarn, work across rem 12 (14, 16) sts and place these sts on holder for right front shoulder.

BUTTONHOLE BAND

Change to smaller needles.
Next row (WS) *P1, k1; rep from * to end. Rep this row once more.

Next (buttonhole) row (WS) Rib 2 sts, [p2tog, yo, rib 3 (4, 5) sts] twice. Cont in rib pat for 2 rows more. Bind off loosely in rib.

Sleeves

With smaller needles and A, cast on 35 (35, 43) sts.

BEG CHART PAT

Row 1 (RS) Beg with st 5 (5, 1) and work to rep line, work 15-st rep once, then work to st 39 (39, 43). Cont to foll chart in this way through row 12. Change to larger needles. Rep rows 1–12 for pat st. AT THE SAME TIME, shape sleeve as foll:
Inc row (RS) K2, M1, work to last 2 sts, M1, k2.
Keeping 2 sts each side as k on RS as established, inc 1 st each side (working new sts in k2, p2 rib) every 6th row 6 (5, 7) times more, then every 4th row 0 (4, 1) times. AT THE SAME TIME, when piece measures approximately 5½ (6, 6½)"/14 (15, 16.5)cm from beg, end with row 2 or 8. Change to B.
Next row (RS) Knit.
Beg with row 4 or 10, cont in chart pat and work even on 49 (55, 61) sts until piece measures 6½ (7, 7½)"/16.5 (18, 19)cm from beg, end with a WS row. Mark beg and end of last row for beg of

sleeve cap. Work even for ½ (¾, ¾)"/1.5 (2, 2)cm, end with a WS row.
Bind off in pat st.

Finishing

Lightly block pieces to measurements. Join right shoulder using 3-needle bind-off.

NECKBAND

With RS facing, smaller needles, and B, pick up and k 5 sts across side edge of buttonhole band, 14 sts along left front neck edge, 12 (13, 13) sts across center front neck edge, 14 sts along right neck edge, 26 (27, 27) sts along back neck edge, then 5 sts across side edge of button band—76 (78, 78) sts.
Next row (WS) *P1, k1; rep from * to end. Rep this row once more.
Next (buttonhole) row (WS) Rib to last 5 sts, p2tog, yo, rib last 3 sts.
Cont in rib pat for 2 rows more. Bind off loosely in rib. Sew on buttons. Button shoulder closed. Sew top edge of sleeve cap to straight edge of armhole, then sew side edges of sleeve cap to bound-off sts of armhole. Sew side and sleeve seams. ■

Pattern for Sleepy Bunny is on page 164.

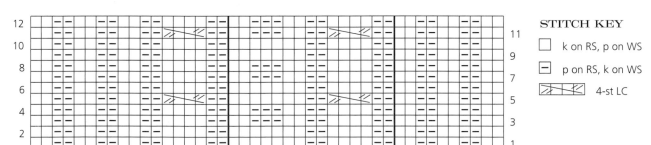

STITCH KEY

☐ k on RS, p on WS

⊟ p on RS, k on WS

4-st LC

162

Sleepy Bunny

Every baby likes to snuggle with a soft friend at naptime—like this plush bunny
who's already drifted off to sleep!

DESIGNED BY GAYLE BUNN

Knitted Measurements
Paw to paw 8"/20.5cm
Tip of ear to tip of toe 12"/30.5cm

Materials
■ 1 3½oz/100g skein (each approx
240yd/220m) of Cascade Yarns
Cherub Aran in #35 taupe (A)

■ Small amounts in #40 black (B)
and #9 ecru (C) for embroidery

■ One pair size 5 (3.75mm) needles
or size to obtain gauge

■ Embroidery needle

■ Stitch holder

■ Stuffing

Bunny Back
FIRST LEG
With A, cast on 13 sts.
Beg with a purl row, work 15 rows in rev
St st (p on RS, k on WS). Break yarn.
Place sts on st holder.

SECOND LEG
Work as for first leg. Do not break yarn.
Leave sts on needle.
Next (joining) row (WS) K 13 sts of 2nd
leg, cast on 10 sts, k 13 sts of first leg
from holder—36 sts.
Work 16 rows more in rev St st.
Next (dec) row (RS) P2tog, p to last 2
sts, p2tog—2 sts dec'd.
Work 5 rows even. Rep dec row once
more—32 sts.
Work 3 rows even.

SHAPE ARMS AND SHOULDERS
Cont in rev St st, cast on 7 sts at beg of
next 2 rows—46 sts.
Work 10 rows even.
Bind off 6 sts at beg of next 4 rows—22 sts.
Work 20 rows even for head.
Next (dec) row (RS) P2tog, p to last 2
sts, p2tog—20 sts.
Work 1 row even.

SHAPE EARS
Next row (RS) P9 and place these sts on
st holder, bind off 2 sts, p9.
Work on rem 9 sts for first ear.
Next (dec) row (WS) K2tog,
k to last 2 sts, k2tog—2 sts dec'd.
Work 2 rows even.
Next (inc) row (RS) Pfb, p to last st,
pfb—9 sts.
Work 14 rows even.
Rep dec row every other row twice
more—5 sts.
Bind off.
Place 9 sts from holder on needle,
ready to work a WS row. Work as for
first ear.

Front
Work as for back.

Finishing
Embroider paws with C and backstitch,
using photo as guide. Embroider face
with B and stem stitch for eyes and
mouth, satin stitch for nose, using
photo as guide. Sew front and back
tog, stuffing head and ears as you sew.
Leave space between legs open until
piece is stuffed as desired. Sew closed. ■

Gauge
22 sts and 28 rows to 4"/10cm over St st using size 5 (3.75mm) needles.
Take time to check gauge.

Slanting Stripes Blanket

Four squares tied together by graphic neutral stripes, with a pop of color
at the border, make a great addition to any modern nursery.

DESIGNED BY SHAINA BILOW

Knitted Measurements
Approx 31½ x 31½"/80 x 80cm

Materials
■ 2 3½oz/100g skeins (each approx 240yd/220m) of Cascade Yarns *Cherub Aran* (nylon/acrylic) each in #01 white (A) and #17 grey (B)

■ One skein each in #40 black (C) and #43 yellow (D)

■ One pair size 6 (4mm) needles *or size to obtain gauge*

■ Size 5 (3.75mm) circular needle, 32"/81cm long

■ Removable stitch markers

Stitch Glossary
kfbf Knit into the front, back, and front of the next st to inc 2 sts.
M1R Insert LH needle from back to front under the strand between last st worked and the next st on the LH needle. Knit into the front loop to twist the st.
M1L Insert the LH needle from front to back under the strand between last st worked and the next st on the LH needle. Knit into the back loop to twist the st.

Stripe Pat 1
76 rows B, [6 rows A, 6 rows C, 6 rows A, 24 rows B] 3 times.

Stripe Pat 2
54 rows A, 24 rows C, 56 rows A, 10 rows B, 10 rows A, 30 rows C, 18 rows A.

Stripe Pat 3
30 rows A, [4 rows A, 4 rows C] 4 times, 20 rows B, 70 rows A, 4 rows C, 4 rows A, 4 rows C, 38 rows A.

Stripe Pat 4
30 rows B, [6 rows C, 4 rows B] twice, 6 rows C, 30 rows B, 30 rows A, 30 rows B, [4 rows C, 4 rows B] 3 times, 4 rows C, 28 rows B.

Note
Blanket is made up of 4 squares, each worked in a different stripe pat. The squares are sewn tog and a border is picked up and worked along each edge.

Blanket
SQUARE
(make 1 foll each stripe pat)
Note Cast-on row is first row of row of stripe pat.
With larger needles and color of first stripe, cast on 1 st.

Set-up row (RS) Kfbf—3 sts.
Next row (WS) Knit.
Next (inc) row (RS) K1, M1L, k to last st, M1R, k1—2 sts inc'd.
Cont in garter st (k every row), rep inc row every other row 48 times more—101 sts.
Work 3 rows even. Place markers each side to mark corners.
Next (dec) row (RS) K1, k2tog, k to last 3 sts, ssk, k1—2 sts dec'd.
Cont in garter st, rep dec row every other row 47 times more—5 sts.
Knit 1 row.
Next row (RS) K1, S2KP, k1—3 sts.
Knit 1 row.
Next row S2KP. Fasten off.

Finishing
Place squares with cast-on st in center. Sew seams from cast-on st to corner marker. With RS facing, D and circular needle, pick up and k 150 sts along 1 edge. Work 6 rows in garter st. Bind off. Rep on opposite edge. With RS facing, D and circular needle, pick up and k 158 sts along one rem edge, including sides of borders already worked. Work 6 rows in garter st, bind off. Rep for opposite edge. ■

Gauge
20 sts and 40 rows to 4"/10cm over garter st using larger needles. *Take time to check gauge.*

Circles & Stripes Set

Your wee one will stand out in a crowd in this charming raglan-sleeve confection, perfect for playing with color.

DESIGNED BY GAYLE BUNN

■■■■

Size
Instructions are written for size 6 months.

Knitted Measurements
SWEATER
Chest 20"/51cm
Length 11"/28cm
Upper arm 9"/23cm

PANTS
Waist (finished) 16"/40.5cm
Length 7"/18cm
Width at hips 21"/53cm

Materials
■ 3 1¾oz/50g skeins (each approx 180yd/165m) of Cascade Yarns *Cherub DK* (nylon/acrylic) in #22 rouge (A)

■ 1 skein each in #06 melon (B) and #40 black (C)

■ One pair each sizes 3 and 4 (3.25 and 3.5mm) needles *or size to obtain gauge*

■ Size 3 (3.25 mm) circular needle, 16"/40cm long

■ Stitch markers, stitch holders

■ Six ¾" (19mm) buttons

■ ½yd (.5mm) of ¾-inch/2cm wide elastic

K1, P1 Rib
(over an odd number of sts)
Row 1 (RS) K1, *p1, k1; rep from * to end.
Row 2 K the knit sts and p the purl sts. Rep row 2 for k1, p1 rib.

Pullover Back
With smaller needles and A, cast on 61 sts. Work in k1, p1 rib for 6 rows. Change to larger needles and, working in St st, foll chart rows 1–36. Cont to foll chart, shape armhole as foll:

SHAPE RAGLAN ARMHOLE
Bind off 2 sts at beg of next 2 rows.
Dec row 39 (RS) K1, k2tog, work to last 3 sts, ssk, k1—2 sts dec'd.
Rep dec row every 4th row twice more, then every other row 12 times—27 sts. Place these sts on a st holder.

Front
Work same as back through row 62 of chart—37 sts.

SHAPE NECK
Row 63 (RS) K1, k2tog, k9, sl next 13 sts to a st holder, join 2nd ball of yarn and k to last 3 sts, ssk, k1.
Cont to work both sides at once with separate balls of yarn, dec 1 st at each neck edge on the next 6 rows, AT THE SAME TIME, dec 1 st at each armhole edge as established 3 times more—2 sts rem each side.
Next row (WS) P2tog each side.
Fasten off.

Right Sleeve
With smaller needles and C, cast on 39 sts. Work in k1, p1 rib for 6 rows. Change to larger needles and work in St st and stripe pat for 2 rows.
Inc 1 st each side of next row, then rep inc every 4th row 7 times more—55 sts. Work even in stripe pat until piece measures 5½"/14cm from beg.

Gauge
24 sts and 30 rows to 4"/10cm over St st using larger needles.
Take time to check gauge.

Circles & Stripes Set

SHAPE RAGLAN CAP
Bind off 5 sts at beg of next RS row, bind off 2 sts at beg of foll (WS) row—48 sts.
Dec row (RS) K1, k2tog, k to last 3 sts, ssk, k1—2 sts dec'd.
Rep dec row every other row 16 times more—14 sts. Place these sts on a st holder.

Left Sleeve
Work same as right sleeve to the raglan cap.

SHAPE RAGLAN CAP
Bind off 2 sts at beg of next RS row, bind off 5 sts at beg of foll (WS) row—48 sts.
Complete as for right sleeve.

Finishing
Sew back raglan seams.

BACK NECKBAND
Note The neckband will be worked across the top of each sleeve and across the back neck edge.
With smaller needles, A, and RS facing, k 14 sts from the sleeve (dec 1 st at center), 27 sts from back neck holder, and 14 sts from the other sleeve (dec 1 st at center)—53 sts. Work in k1, p1 rib for 7 rows. Bind off in rib.

FRONT NECKBAND
With smaller needles, A, and RS facing, pick up and k 11 sts from shaped neck edge, 13 sts from neck holder, 11 sts from shaped neck edge—35 sts.
Work in k1, p1 rib for 7 rows. Bind off in rib.

RIGHT RAGLAN BUTTONHOLE BAND
With smaller needles and C, pick up and k 37 sts along right front raglan seam edge. Work in k1, p1 rib for 3 rows.

Buttonhole row (RS) Rib 3 [bind off 2 sts, rib until there are 9 sts] twice, bind off 2 sts, rib 10.
Next row Work in rib, casting on 2 sts over each set of bound-off sts. Work 2 more rows in rib. Bind off in rib.

LEFT RAGLAN BUTTONHOLE BAND
Work same as right front band for 3 rows.
Buttonhole row (RS) Rib 10, [bind off 2 sts, rib until there are 9 sts] twice, bind off 2 sts, rib to end. Complete as for right band.

BACK RAGLAN BUTTON BANDS
Work 7 rows as for front buttonhole bands, only without buttonhole. Sew buttonhole band to button band at the base of each band. Sew side and sleeve seams. Sew on buttons.

Pants—Left Leg
Note Chart for the right leg is a mirror image of the left leg.

FIRST SIDE
With larger needles and A, cast on 7 sts.
Row 1 P7.
Row 2 K7.
Row 3 Cast on 9 sts, p to end.
Row 4 Bind off 2 sts, k to end—14 sts.
Row 5 Cast on 9 sts, p to end—23 sts.
Leave these sts on a spare needle.

SECOND SIDE
With larger needles and A, cast on 7 sts.
Row 1 K7.
Row 2 P7.
Row 3 Cast on 9 sts, k to end.
Row 4 Bind off 2 sts, p to end—14 sts.

Row 5 Cast on 9 sts, k to end—23 sts.
Row 6 P23, cast on 25 sts, p 23 sts of first side—71 sts.
The sts are set up to beg working the chart.

BEG CHART PATTERN
Rows 1 and 2 With A, foll chart, knit 1 row, purl 1 row.
Row 3 (dec) K2tog, k to last 2 sts, k2tog—2 sts dec'd.
Row 4 Purl.
Row 5 (dec) Rep dec row 3—67 sts.
Rows 6–36 Work even, foll chart.**

SHAPE BACK
Keeping to chart pat, work as foll:
Row 37 (RS) K52, turn and leave rem sts unworked.
Row 38 P52.
Row 39 K37, turn.
Row 40 P37.
Row 41 K22, turn.
Row 42 P22.
Row 43 K7. Break A and place all sts on a st holder.

Right Leg
Work as for left leg to **—67 sts.

SHAPE BACK
Keeping to chart pat, work as foll:
Next row (RS) Knit.
Next row P52, turn and leave rem sts unworked.
Next row K52.
Next row P37, turn.
Next row K37.
Next row P22, turn.
Next row K22.
Next row P7. Place all sts on st holder.

PULLOVER

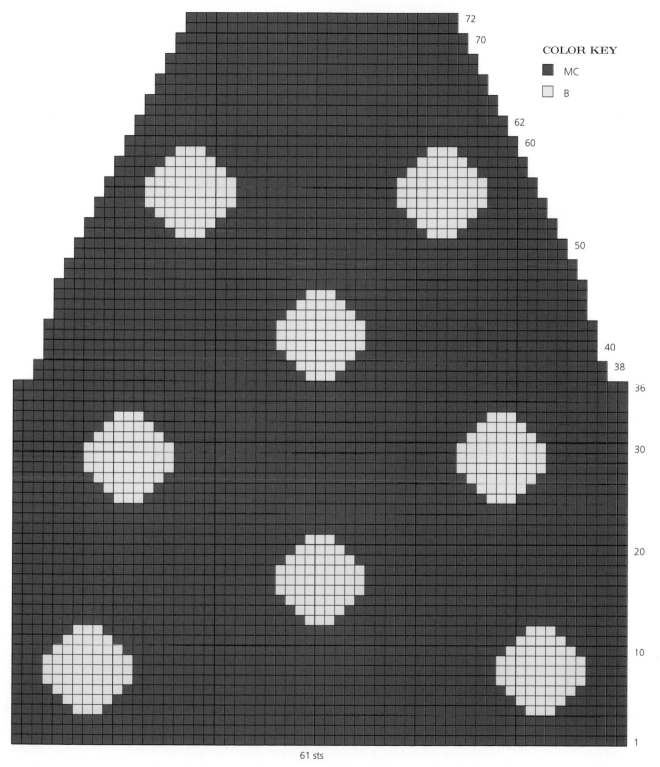

72
70
62
60
50
40
38
36
30
20
10
1

COLOR KEY
MC
B

61 sts

54 Circles & Stripes Set

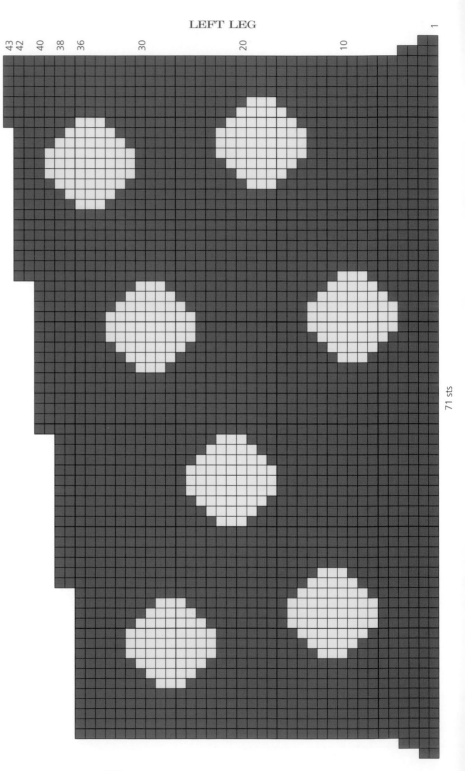

Finishing
LEG CUFF
With smaller needles and A, pick up
and k 59 sts along one leg edge. Work
in k1, p1 rib for 2"/5cm. Bind off in rib.
Rep for other leg.
Sew inner leg and crotch seams. Fold
leg cuff to WS and sew in place.

WAISTBAND
With circular needle and A, beg at
center back seam, work sts as foll:
[k2tog, k14] 4 times, then k1, k2tog
from left leg, then [k2tog, k14] 4 times,
k1, k2tog from right leg—124 sts.
Join to work in rnds and place marker
for beg of rnd. Work in rnds of k1, p1
rib for 2½"/6.5cm. Bind off in rib.
Sew waistband to WS, leaving an
opening for the elastic. Cut elastic to
fit waist measurements and pull
through opening. Secure ends and close
up opening. ■

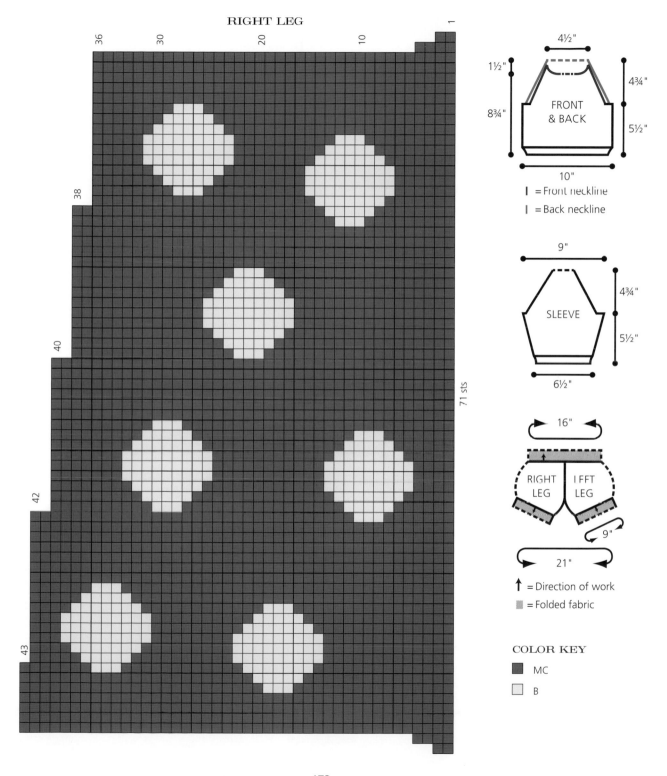

RIGHT LEG

1
10
20
30
36
38
40
42
43

71 sts

4½"

1½"

8¾"

FRONT
& BACK

4¾"

5½"

10"

I = Front neckline

I = Back neckline

9"

SLEEVE

4¾"

5½"

6½"

16"

RIGHT
LEG

LEFT
LEG

9"

21"

↑ = Direction of work

■ = Folded fabric

COLOR KEY

■ MC

☐ B

55

Garter Stitch Hoodie

A thick garter stitch fabric and snuggly hood will keep baby warm all winter, inside and out.

DESIGNED BY SANDI PROSSER

■■□□

Sizes
Instructions are written for size 3 months (6 months, 12 months). Shown in size 6 months.

Knitted Measurements
Chest 20 (21, 22)"/51 (53, 56)cm
Length 10 (11, 12)"/25.5 (28, 30.5)cm
Upper arm 8½ (9½, 10½)"/21.5 (24, 26.5)cm

Materials
■ 2 3½oz/100g skeins (each approx 240yd/220m) of Cascade Yarns *Cherub Aran* (nylon/acrylic) in #19 geranium (MC)

■ 1 skein in #22 rouge (CC)

■ One pair size 7 (4.5mm) needles *or size to obtain gauge*

Back
With MC, cast on 54 (58, 62) sts. Beg with a WS row, work in garter st (knit every row) until piece measures 5¾ (6¼, 6¾)"/14.5 (16, 17)cm from beg, end with a WS row. Break MC and join CC. Cont even in garter st, with CC, until piece measures 10 (11, 12)"/25.5 (28, 30.5)cm from beg, end with a WS row. Bind off.

Front
Work as for back until piece measures 7½ (8½, 9½)"/19 (21.5, 24)cm from beg, end with a WS row.

SHAPE NECK
Next row (RS) K20 (22, 24), join a 2nd ball of yarn and bind off center 14 sts, knit to end of row.
Working both sides at once with separate balls of yarn, dec 1 st at each neck edge *every* row 3 times, then *every other* row 4 times—13 (15, 17) sts rem each side for shoulder.
Work even until piece measures same as back, end with a WS row. Bind off rem sts each side.

Sleeves
With CC, cast on 33 (35, 38) sts. Beg with a WS row, work 19 rows in garter st.
Next (inc) row (RS) K1, M1, knit to last st, M1, k1—2 sts inc'd.
Rep inc row every 6th row 6 (8, 9) times more—47 (53, 58) sts. Work even until piece measures 7 (7½, 8)"/18 (19, 20.5)cm, end with a WS row. Bind off.

Gauge
22 sts and 40 rows to 4"/10cm over garter stitch using size 7 (4.5mm) needles. *Take time to check gauge.*

55

Garter Stitch Hoodie

Hood

With MC, cast on 88 sts. Beg with a
WS row, work in garter st for
2½"/6.5cm, end with a WS row.
Break MC and join CC. Knit 2 rows.
Next (dec) row (RS) K1, k2tog, knit
to last 3 sts, ssk, k1—2 sts dec'd.
Rep dec row every 4th row 3 times
more—80 sts.
Work even until piece measures
6½"/16.5cm from beg, end with a
WS row.

SHAPE BACK

Bind off 7 sts at beg of next 10 rows.
Bind off rem 10 sts.

Finishing

Sew shoulder seams. Fold hood
in half and sew shaped back seam. Sew
hood to neck opening, having cast-on
edges meeting at center front and back
seam aligned with center back. Sew in
sleeves. Sew side and sleeve seams,
reversing seaming 1½"/4cm from sleeve
cast-on edge to allow for turnback. ■

✳
Pattern for
All About Aran
pants is on
page 40.

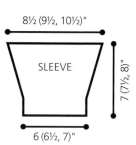

8½ (9½, 10½)"

SLEEVE

7 (7½, 8)"

6 (6½, 7)"

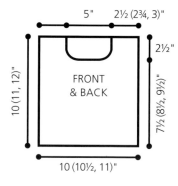

5"   2½ (2¾, 3)"

2½"

FRONT
& BACK

10 (11, 12)"

7½ (8½, 9½)"

10 (10½, 11)"

Plaid Earflap Cap

This sporty and super-cute topper keeps a little head cozy with earflaps, I-cord ties, and a crocheted visor.

DESIGNED BY KRISTIN EKSUSIAN

Size
Instructions are written for one size, to fit baby.

Knitted Measurements
Head circumference 14"/35.5cm
Length excluding earflaps 6"/15cm

Materials
■ 1 3½oz/100g skein (each approx 240yd/220m) of Cascade Yarns *Cherub Aran* (nylon/acrylic) each in #40 black (A) and #25 ruby (B)

■ One set (5) size 7 (4.5mm) double-pointed needles (dpns) *or size to obtain gauge*

■ Size H/8 (5mm) crochet hook

■ 4 removable stitch markers, 1 closed stitch marker

Stitch Glossary
sc Single crochet.
hdc Half double crochet.

Cap
With A, cast on 70 sts. Join, being careful not to twist sts, and place marker (pm) for beg of rnd. Work set-up rnd, placing markers in cast-on st below last st worked as foll:

Set-up rnd K9, pm, k15 (left earflap), pm, k23, k15 (right earflap), pm, k to end of rnd.
Work in garter st (p 1 rnd, k 1 rnd) until piece measures 1"/2.5cm from beg, end with a purl rnd.

BEGIN CHART
Rnd 1 Work 10-st rep 7 times around. Cont to work chart in this manner, noting that crown shaping begins in rnd 24 and all k2togs are worked in A. When rnd 32 is complete, break yarn, leaving long tails. Thread the A tail through the rem 7 sts and pull tightly to close.

Gauge
20 sts and 26 rnds to 4"/10cm over chart pat using size 7 (4.5mm) needles. *Take time to check gauge.*

Plaid Earflap Cap

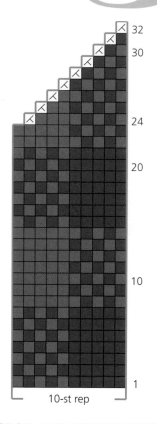

32
30
24
20
10
1

10-st rep

COLOR AND STITCH KEY

■ A

■ B

☒ k2tog with A

Earflaps

With RS facing and A, pick up and k 15 sts between markers for left earflap. Work in garter st (k every row) for 9 rows more.

Next (dec) row (RS) K1, ssk, k to last 3 sts, k2tog, k1—2 sts dec'd.
Rep dec row every row 4 times more— 5 sts.
Next row Ssk, k1, k2tog—3 sts.
Next (I-cord) row *K3, slide sts to opposite end of needle to knit next row from RS, pulling yarn tightly across back of work; rep from * until cord measures 8"/12.5cm. Break yarn, leaving a long tail. Thread tail through open sts.
Rep for right earflap.

Visor

With A and crochet hook, join with slip st to 3rd st from right earflap.
Next row *2 sc in next st, 1 sc in foll st; rep from * until 3 sts rem before left ear flap, sl st in next st. Ch 2, turn.
Next row *Hdc in next sc; rep from * to last st, slip st in last st, slip st in next cast-on st. Ch 1, turn.
Next row Sc in each hdc across, slip st in next st. Do not turn.
Work 1 rnd of sc around entire edge of cap, including earflaps.
Work 1 row more of sc along edge of visor, slip st in st before left earflap.
Fasten off. ■

Railroad Cap

This charming choo-choo is created with a combination of Fair Isle and duplicate stitch, with a variegated colorway painting the sky.

DESIGNED BY PAT OLSKI

Size
Instructions are written for one size, to fit baby.

Knitted Measurements
Head circumference 14"/35.5cm
Length 7"/18cm

Materials
■ 1 3½oz/100g skein (each approx 240yd/220m) of Cascade Yarns *Cherub Aran* (nylon/acrylic) in #08 baby blues (A), #40 black (B), #25 ruby (C), and #21 grass (D)

■ One set (5) each sizes 4 and 6 (3.5 and 4mm) double-pointed needles (dpns) *or size to obtain gauge*

■ Stitch marker

■ Tapestry needle

Hat
With smaller needles and D, cast on 80 sts. Join, being careful not to twist sts, and pm for beg of rnd.
Next rnd *K2, p2; rep from * around for k2, p2 rib.
Cont in k2, p2 rib until piece measures 1"/2.5cm from beg. Break D.
Change to larger needles.

BEGIN TRACK PAT
Rnd 1 With B, knit.
Rnds 2 and 3 *K1 B, k3 A; rep from * around.
Rep rnds 1–3 once more, then rep rnd 1.

BEGIN CHART
Note that piece is worked using 2 colors in each chart rnd. When 3 colors are needed, the 3rd color is added using duplicate st in finishing. The roof of the engine in rnds 12 and 13 is also added using duplicate st.
Rnd 1 Work to rep line, work 10-st rep 5 times around.
Cont to work chart in this way until rnd 11 is complete.
Break B and C and cont with A only to end of hat.

SHAPE CROWN
With A, work in St st until piece measures 5½"/14cm from beg.
Next (dec) rnd [K7, k2tog] 8 times around, k8—72 sts.
Next (dec) rnd [K6, k2tog] 9 times around—63 sts.
Next (dec) rnd [K5, k2tog] 9 times around—54 sts.
Cont in this manner, working 1 less st before the k2tog, every rnd until 18 sts rem.
Next rnd [K2tog] 9 times around.
Break yarn, leaving a long tail. Thread tail through rem 9 sts and pull tightly to close.

Finishing
Block lightly if necessary. With tapestry needle and 1 strand of yarn, foll chart for duplicate st embroidery. With tapestry needle and 1 strand of B, work straight sts to border the 2 wheels of the caboose and the small wheel of the engine ■.

Gauge
23 sts and 26 rnds to 4"/10cm over chart pat using larger needles.
Take time to check gauge.

Railroad Cap

COLOR AND STITCH KEY

☐	A
■	B
■	C
☒	duplicate stitch with A
V	duplicate stitch with B

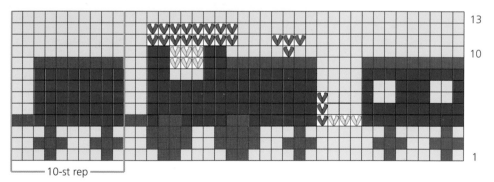

← 10-st rep →

13

10

1

58

Whale Vest

A chevron stripe evokes waves under a smiling creature
of the sea, worked in intarsia and duplicate stitch.

DESIGNED BY SANDI PROSSER

Sizes
Instructions are written for size 3 months
(6 months, 12 months). Shown in size 6
months.

Knitted Measurements
Chest 18 (20, 23)"/45.5 (51, 58.5)cm
Length 9½ (10½, 11½)"/24 (26.5, 29)cm

Materials
■ 2 1¾oz/50g skeins (each approx
180yd/165m) of Cascade Yarns
Cherub DK (nylon/acrylic) in #48
methyl blue (MC)
■ 1 skein in #9 ecru (CC)
■ One pair each sizes 3 and 4 (3.25 and
3.5mm) needles *or size to obtain gauge*
■ Size 3 (3.25mm) circular needle,
24"/60cm long
■ Stitch holders

K2, P2 Rib
(multiple of 4 sts plus 2)
Row 1 (RS) K2, *p2, k2; rep from
* to end.
Row 2 K the knit sts and p the purl sts.
Rep row 2 for k2, p2 rib.

Notes
1) For whale chart pat, use a separate
bobbin (or strand) of color for each
color section.
2) Mouth and spray are each
worked in duplicate stitch after knitting
is completed.
3) When changing colors, pick up
new color from under dropped color
to prevent holes.

Back
With smaller needles and MC, cast on
62 (70, 78) sts. Work in k2, p2 rib for
8 (10, 12) rows, inc (dec, dec) 1 st in
center of last row and end with a WS
row—63 (69, 77) sts. Change to larger
needles and St st (k on RS, p on WS).
Work even for 2 rows, end with a
WS row.

BEG CHART 1
Row 1 (RS) Beg with st 1 (1, 3) and work
to rep line, work 6-st rep 9 (10, 12)
times, then work through st 15 (15, 13).
Cont to foll chart in this way through
row 5. With MC only, work even until
piece measures 5½ (6, 6½)"/14 (15,
16.5)cm from beg, end with a WS row.

ARMHOLE SHAPING
Bind off 3 (4, 6) sts at beg of next 2 rows.
Row 1 (dec RS) K1, k2tog, knit to last
3 sts, ssk, k1.
Row 2 (dec) P1, p2tog tbl, purl to last
3 sts, p2tog, p1.
Row 3 (dec) K1, k2tog, knit to last 3 sts,
ssk, k1.
Row 4 Purl.
Rep rows 3 and 4 three times more—45
(49, 53) sts.

Gauge
27 sts and 35 rows to 4"/10cm over St st using larger needles.
Take time to check gauge.

Work even until armhole measures 4 (4½, 5)"/10 (11.5, 12.5)cm, end with a WS row.

SHOULDER SHAPING
Bind off 10 (11, 12) sts at beg of next 2 rows. Place rem 25 (27, 29) sts on holder for back neck.

Front
Work as for back until chart 1 is complete, end with a RS row. With MC only, work even for 3 rows, end with a WS row.

BEG CHART 2
Row 1 (RS) With MC, k11 (14, 18), work 40 sts of chart, with MC, k12 (15, 19). Cont to foll chart in this way through row 24. With MC only, work even until piece measures same length as back to underarm, end with a WS row. Shape armholes same as back, AT THE SAME TIME, when armhole measures ½"/1.5cm, end with a WS row.

NECK SHAPING
Next row (RS) Work across to center st, place center st on holder; join a 2nd ball of MC, work to end. Working both sides at once, purl next row.
Next (dec) row (RS) With first ball of yarn, work to last 3 sts, k2tog, k1; with 2nd ball of yarn, k1, ssk, work to end. Purl next row. Rep last 2 rows 11 (12, 13) times more—10 (11, 12) sts each side. Work even until piece measures same length as back to shoulder, end with a WS row. Bind off each side.

Finishing
Lightly block pieces to measurements.

EMBROIDERY
Referring to chart 2, embroider duplicate stitch mouth and eye using MC and spray using CC. Sew shoulder seams.

NECKBAND
With RS facing, circular needle, and MC, pick up and k 36 (39, 42) sts evenly spaced along right front neck edge to right shoulder seam, k 25 (27, 29) sts from back neck holder, pick up and k 36 (39, 42) sts evenly spaced along left front neck edge, then k 1 st from front holder—98 (106, 114) sts. Do not join. Work back and forth as foll:
Row 1 (WS) With MC, p2, *k2, p2; rep from * to end.
Row 2 With CC, knit.
Row 3 With CC, p2, *k2, p2; rep from * to end.
Row 4 With MC, knit.
Row 5 With MC, p2, *k2, p2; rep from * to end. With MC, bind off loosely in rib. Lap side edge of right neckband over side edge of left neckband, then sew side edges in place.

ARMBANDS
With RS facing, smaller needles, and MC, pick up and k 70 (78, 86) sts evenly spaced along entire armhole edge. Rep rows 1–5 as for neckband. With MC, bind off loosely in rib. Sew side and armband seams. ∎

Whale Vest

CHART 2

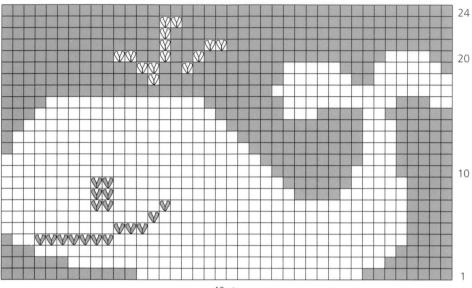

40 sts

CHART 1

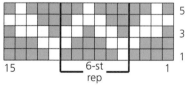

15   6-st   1
rep

COLOR AND STITCH KEY

  MC

☐ CC

  duplicate stitch over CC with MC

Ⓥ duplicate stitch over MC with CC

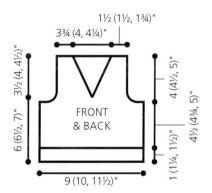

59

Merry Monsters

With striped limbs and hair, rolled eye sockets, and a cute button nose,
these monsters are more sweet than scary!

DESIGNED BY CHARLES GANDY

Knitted Measurements
Circumference (stuffed) 7½ (9)"/19 (23)cm
Length (excluding appendages and legs) 6 (9)"/15 (23)cm

Materials
■ 1 3½oz/100g skein (each approx 240yd/220m) of Cascade Yarns *Cherub Aran* (nylon/acrylic) each in #01 white (A), #22 rouge (B), #14 melon (C), and #30 violet (D)

■ 2 sets (5 each) size 4 (3.5mm) double-pointed needles (dpns) *or size to obtain gauge*

■ Scrap yarn and crochet hook for provisional cast-on

■ Stitch markers

■ Fiberfill stuffing

Provisional Cast-On
With scrap yarn and crochet hook, chain the number of sts to cast on plus a few extra. Cut a tail and pull the tail through the last chain. With knitting needle and yarn, pick up and knit the stated number of sts through the "bumps" on the back of the chain. To remove scrap yarn chain, when instructed, pull out the tail from the last crochet stitch. Gently and slowly pull on the tail to unravel the crochet stitches, carefully placing each released knit stitch on a needle.

Notes
1) Placement and color of stripes is random and as desired.
2) Knots are used when joining new colors for extra stability. Tie the new color in, leaving a long tail to weave in before stuffing.

Little Monster (Big Monster) Body
Using provisional cast-on method and A, cast on 30 (40) sts. Join, being careful not to twist sts, and place marker (pm) for beg of rnd. Work in St st (k every rnd) for 3 (6)"/7.5 (15)cm.

DIVIDE FOR FRONT AND BACK
Cont in St st in rows (k on RS, p on WS) on first 15 (20) sts only for back for ¾ (1)"/2 (2.5)cm more. Place these sts on a spare needle.
Join yarn to rem 15 (20) sts for front, and work in St st on these sts only for ½ (¾)"/1.5 (2)cm.
Set body aside.

Gauge
22 sts and 28 rows/rnds to 4"/10cm over St st using size 4 (3.5mm) needles.
Take time to check gauge.

Merry Monsters

Eye Sockets (make 2)
With B, cast on 10 (14) sts. Join, being careful not to twist sts, and pm for beg of rnd. Work 12 rnds in St st.

JOIN BASE OF EYE SOCKET
Divide sts evenly on 2 dpns. With a 3rd dpn, *k 1 st from first needle tog with 1 st from 2nd needle; rep from * until all sts have been joined—5 (7) sts. Set socket aside.

Nose
Using provisional cast-on method and A, cast on 10 (12) sts. Join, being careful not to twist sts, and pm for beg of rnd. Work in St st for 1 (1½)"/2.5 (4)cm.

JOIN TOP OF NOSE
Divide sts evenly on 2 dpns. With a 3rd dpn, *k 1 st from first needle tog with 1 st from 2nd needle; rep from * until all sts have been joined—5 (6) sts. Set nose aside.

JOIN NOSE AND EYE SOCKETS TO BODY
With A, hold sts for 1 eye socket in front of sts for front of body.
Next row *K 1 st from first needle tog with 1 st from 2nd needle; rep from * until all sts of eye socket have been joined.
Join nose, and then 2nd eye socket in same way.
Cont to work in St st on sts for front until front measures same as back.
Next rnd Work 15 (20) sts for front, work 15 (20) sts for back, pm for beg of rnd.
Cont to work in St st over 30 (40) sts for body until piece measures 6 (9)"/15 (23)cm from beg.

Hair
1ST LOCK
Next rnd K3 (4), place next 12 (16) sts on 1 dpn to hold for front, place next 12 (16) sts on 2nd dpn to hold for back, cast on 1 st, k rem 3 (4) sts, pm for beg of rnd—7 (9) sts.
Work even on these 7 (9) sts, changing colors for stripes as desired, until lock measures approx 2 (3)"/5 (7.5)cm. Break yarn and thread tail through sts to close.

2ND LOCK
Next rnd K 3 (4) sts from front dpn, cast on 2 sts, k 3 (4) sts from back dpn, pick up and k 2 sts along cast-on sts of 1st lock—10 (12) sts. Complete as for 1st lock.

Work 3 additional locks in this manner, varying the heights as desired and varying the thickness of the locks by casting on and picking up more or fewer sts between locks.

ARMS
With A, pick up and k 6 (8) sts along side of opening on back of face, pick up and k 2 sts in gap between front and back, pick up and k 6 (8) sts along side of opening on front of face, pick up and k 2 sts in gap between front and back, pm for beg of rnd—16 (20) sts.
Work in St st, changing colors for stripes as desired, until arm is desired length. Break yarn and thread tail through sts to close.

BEGIN STUFFING
Weave in ends. Stuff each hair lock, varying the size by stuffing more or less. Stuff the arms as desired and most of the body.

LEGS
Remove provisional cast-on, placing 5 (7) sts from right front on a dpn, and 5 sts from right back on a 2nd dpn—10 (14) sts. Place rem sts on spare dpns to hold.
Divide the 10 (14) leg sts on 3 dpns and work even, changing colors for stripes as desired, for approx 1½ (2)"/4 (5)cm. Close as for arms. Rep for 2nd leg, leaving center sts on hold. Bind off center sts on each side.

Finishing
EYEBALLS (MAKE 2)
With D, cast on 6 (9) sts. Work in St st in rows until piece measures ¾ (1)"/2 (2.5)cm from beg. Break yarn, leaving a long tail. Weave tail through rem sts and sew around the edges. Stuff lightly and cinch closed, forming a small ball. Sew ball to center of eye socket.
Stuff nose and close as for arms.
Tack down to body if desired. Finish stuffing body and legs. Sew seam between legs. ■

60

Bow Beret

Your favorite little girl will love this darling hat with a contrasting bow and tromp l'oeil ribbon around the brim.

DESIGNED BY JESSE MOLZAN

Size

Instructions are written for one size, to fit baby.

Knitted Measurements

Brim circumference 14"/35.5cm
Length 7"/18cm

Materials

■ 1 3½oz/100g skein (each approx 240yd/220m) of Cascade Yarns *Cherub Aran* (nylon/acrylic) in #25 ruby (A)

■ Small amount in #45 raspberry (B)

■ One set (5) size 6 (4mm) double-pointed needles (dpns) *or size to obtain gauge*

■ Stitch marker

Beret

With A, cast on 84 sts. Join, being careful not to twist sts, and place marker for beg of rnd.
Next rnd *K2, p2; rep from * around for k2, p2 rib.
Cont in k2, p2 rib for 3 rnds more.
Knit 3 rnds.

BEGIN FAIR ISLE BORDER

Next (border) rnd *K4 B, k2 A; rep from * around.
Rep border rnd twice more. Break B.
Next (inc) rnd With A, [kfb] twice, k to end of rnd—86 sts.
Knit 1 rnd.
Next (inc) rnd *K1, kfb; rep from * around—129 sts.
Work even until piece measures 5½"/14cm from beg.

SHAPE CROWN

Next (dec) rnd *K2tog, k1; rep from * around—86 sts.
Knit 1 rnd.
Next (dec) rnd *K2tog, k1; rep from * to last 2 sts, k2tog—57 sts.
Knit 2 rnds.
Next (dec) rnd *K2tog, k1; rep from * around—38 sts.
Knit 1 rnd.
Next (dec) rnd *K2tog, k1; rep from * to last 2 sts, k2tog—25 sts.
Knit 1 rnd. Break yarn, leaving a long tail.
Thread tail through rem sts and pull tight to close.

Bow

With B, cast on 12 sts.
Row 1 (RS) *K1, p1; rep from * across.
Row 2 K the purl sts and p the knit sts as they appear for seed st.
Cont in seed st until piece measures 3½"/9cm from beg. Bind off.
Break yarn.
Pinch piece at center and run a strand of B through center to form bow.
With A, using photo as guide, attach bow to hat. ■

Gauge

22 sts and 28 rnds to 4"/10cm over St st using size 6 (4mm) needles.
Take time to check gauge.

Pattern for
Mini Mackintosh
is on page 74.

index